D1571317

About the Reader

NAME ....

FAVORITE BOOK ....

FAVORITE AUTHOR ....

FAVORITE GENRE ....

BOOKS TO READ

Book Review

TITLE ....

AUTHOR ....

SERIES ....

SERIES BOOK # .... PAGE COUNT ....

GENRE ....

FORMAT ....

START DATE .... FINISH DATE ....

☆☆☆☆☆

PLOT

THOUGHTS

QUOTES

Book Review

TITLE ....

AUTHOR ....

SERIES ....

SERIES BOOK # .... PAGE COUNT ....

GENRE ....

FORMAT ....

START DATE .... FINISH DATE ....

☆☆☆☆☆

PLOT

_____

THOUGHTS

_____

QUOTES

Book Review

TITLE ....

AUTHOR ....

SERIES...

SERIES BOOK #............. PAGE COUNT...............

GENRE..

FORMAT..

START DATE................. FINISH DATE ....

☆☆☆☆☆

PLOT

___

THOUGHTS

___

QUOTES

Book Review

TITLE ....

AUTHOR ....

SERIES..

SERIES BOOK #.............. PAGE COUNT..............

GENRE...

FORMAT...

START DATE................. FINISH DATE ....

☆☆☆☆☆

PLOT

THOUGHTS

QUOTES

Book Review

TITLE ....

AUTHOR ....

SERIES...

SERIES BOOK #............. PAGE COUNT...............

GENRE..

FORMAT..

START DATE................ FINISH DATE ....

☆☆☆☆☆

PLOT

THOUGHTS

QUOTES

Book Review

TITLE ....

AUTHOR ....

SERIES..

SERIES BOOK #............... PAGE COUNT...............

GENRE...

FORMAT..

START DATE................. FINISH DATE ....

☆☆☆☆☆

PLOT

THOUGHTS

QUOTES

Book Review

TITLE ....

AUTHOR ....

SERIES..

SERIES BOOK #.............. PAGE COUNT................

GENRE...

FORMAT...

START DATE................. FINISH DATE ....

☆☆☆☆☆

PLOT

THOUGHTS

QUOTES

Book Review

TITLE ....

AUTHOR ....

SERIES..

SERIES BOOK #................ PAGE COUNT................

GENRE ....

FORMAT...

START DATE................ FINISH DATE ....

☆☆☆☆☆

PLOT

THOUGHTS

QUOTES

Book Review

TITLE ....

AUTHOR ....

SERIES...

SERIES BOOK #.............. PAGE COUNT.................

GENRE...

FORMAT..

START DATE.................. FINISH DATE ....

☆☆☆☆☆

PLOT

THOUGHTS

QUOTES

Book Review

TITLE ....

AUTHOR ....

SERIES...

SERIES BOOK #............... PAGE COUNT.................

GENRE...

FORMAT...

START DATE.................. FINISH DATE ....

☆☆☆☆☆

PLOT

THOUGHTS

QUOTES

Book Review

TITLE ....

AUTHOR ....

SERIES ....

SERIES BOOK # .... PAGE COUNT ....

GENRE ....

FORMAT ....

START DATE .... FINISH DATE ....

☆☆☆☆☆

PLOT

THOUGHTS

QUOTES

Book Review

TITLE ....

AUTHOR ....

SERIES..

SERIES BOOK #................ PAGE COUNT...............

GENRE..

FORMAT..

START DATE................. FINISH DATE ....

☆☆☆☆☆

PLOT

THOUGHTS

QUOTES

Book Review

TITLE ....

AUTHOR ....

SERIES...

SERIES BOOK #............... PAGE COUNT...............

GENRE..

FORMAT...

START DATE................. FINISH DATE ....

☆☆☆☆☆

PLOT

THOUGHTS

QUOTES

Book Review

TITLE ....

AUTHOR ....

SERIES..

SERIES BOOK #.............. PAGE COUNT.................

GENRE..

FORMAT...

START DATE................. FINISH DATE ....

☆☆☆☆☆

PLOT

_____

THOUGHTS

_____

QUOTES

Book Review

TITLE ....

AUTHOR ....

SERIES...

SERIES BOOK # .... PAGE COUNT................

GENRE...

FORMAT...

START DATE................. FINISH DATE ....

☆☆☆☆☆

PLOT

THOUGHTS

QUOTES

Book Review

TITLE ....

AUTHOR ....

SERIES ....

SERIES BOOK #............... PAGE COUNT...............

GENRE ....

FORMAT ....

START DATE................. FINISH DATE ....

☆☆☆☆☆

PLOT

THOUGHTS

QUOTES

Book Review

TITLE ....

AUTHOR ....

SERIES ....

SERIES BOOK # .... PAGE COUNT ....

GENRE ....

FORMAT ....

START DATE .... FINISH DATE ....

☆☆☆☆☆

PLOT

_____

THOUGHTS

_____

QUOTES

Book Review

TITLE ....

AUTHOR ....

SERIES...

SERIES BOOK #................. PAGE COUNT................

GENRE...

FORMAT..

START DATE................. FINISH DATE ....

☆☆☆☆☆

PLOT

THOUGHTS

QUOTES

Book Review

TITLE ....

AUTHOR ....

SERIES...

SERIES BOOK #................. PAGE COUNT...................

GENRE...

FORMAT...

START DATE................. FINISH DATE ....

☆☆☆☆☆

PLOT

THOUGHTS

QUOTES

Book Review

TITLE ....

AUTHOR ....

SERIES..

SERIES BOOK #................ PAGE COUNT................

GENRE..

FORMAT..

START DATE.................. FINISH DATE ....

☆☆☆☆☆

PLOT

THOUGHTS

QUOTES

Book Review

TITLE ....

AUTHOR ....

SERIES...

SERIES BOOK #................ PAGE COUNT.................

GENRE...

FORMAT..

START DATE................. FINISH DATE ....

☆☆☆☆☆

PLOT

THOUGHTS

QUOTES

Book Review

TITLE ....

AUTHOR ....

SERIES...

SERIES BOOK #.............. PAGE COUNT.................

GENRE..

FORMAT...

START DATE................. FINISH DATE ....

☆☆☆☆☆

PLOT

THOUGHTS

QUOTES

Book Review

TITLE ....

AUTHOR ....

SERIES..

SERIES BOOK # .... PAGE COUNT ....

GENRE ....

FORMAT ....

START DATE .... FINISH DATE ....

☆☆☆☆☆

PLOT

THOUGHTS

QUOTES

Book Review

TITLE ....

AUTHOR ....

SERIES ....

SERIES BOOK # .... PAGE COUNT ....

GENRE ....

FORMAT ....

START DATE .... FINISH DATE ....

☆☆☆☆☆

PLOT

THOUGHTS

QUOTES

Book Review

TITLE ....

AUTHOR ....

SERIES...

SERIES BOOK #................ PAGE COUNT................

GENRE...

FORMAT...

START DATE................. FINISH DATE ....

☆☆☆☆☆

PLOT

THOUGHTS

QUOTES

Book Review

TITLE ....

AUTHOR ....

SERIES..

SERIES BOOK #................ PAGE COUNT...............

GENRE..

FORMAT..

START DATE................ FINISH DATE ....

☆☆☆☆☆

PLOT

THOUGHTS

QUOTES

Book Review

TITLE ....

AUTHOR ....

SERIES...

SERIES BOOK #............. PAGE COUNT.............

GENRE...

FORMAT...

START DATE................. FINISH DATE ....

☆☆☆☆☆

PLOT

THOUGHTS

QUOTES

Book Review

TITLE ....

AUTHOR ....

SERIES...

SERIES BOOK #............... PAGE COUNT...............

GENRE...

FORMAT..

START DATE................. FINISH DATE ....

☆☆☆☆☆

PLOT

THOUGHTS

QUOTES

Book Review

TITLE ....

AUTHOR ....

SERIES ....

SERIES BOOK # .... PAGE COUNT ....

GENRE ....

FORMAT ....

START DATE .... FINISH DATE ....

☆☆☆☆☆

PLOT

THOUGHTS

QUOTES

Book Review

TITLE ....

AUTHOR ....

SERIES...

SERIES BOOK #................ PAGE COUNT................

GENRE..

FORMAT...

START DATE.................. FINISH DATE ....

☆☆☆☆☆

PLOT

___

THOUGHTS

___

QUOTES

Book Review

TITLE ....

AUTHOR ....

SERIES..

SERIES BOOK # .... PAGE COUNT................

GENRE..

FORMAT...

START DATE.................. FINISH DATE ....

☆☆☆☆☆

PLOT

THOUGHTS

QUOTES

Book Review

TITLE ....

AUTHOR ....

SERIES...

SERIES BOOK #............... PAGE COUNT.................

GENRE..

FORMAT..

START DATE................ FINISH DATE ....

☆☆☆☆☆

PLOT

___

THOUGHTS

___

QUOTES

Book Review

TITLE ....

AUTHOR ....

SERIES...

SERIES BOOK #............... PAGE COUNT...............

GENRE...

FORMAT..

START DATE.................. FINISH DATE ....

☆☆☆☆☆

PLOT

THOUGHTS

QUOTES

Book Review

TITLE ....

AUTHOR ....

SERIES...

SERIES BOOK #.............. PAGE COUNT...............

GENRE...

FORMAT...

START DATE................. FINISH DATE ....

☆☆☆☆☆

PLOT

THOUGHTS

QUOTES

Book Review

TITLE ....

AUTHOR ....

SERIES..

SERIES BOOK #............ PAGE COUNT...............

GENRE..

FORMAT..

START DATE................. FINISH DATE ....

☆☆☆☆☆

PLOT

THOUGHTS

QUOTES

Book Review

TITLE ....

AUTHOR ....

SERIES...

SERIES BOOK #.............. PAGE COUNT...............

GENRE..

FORMAT..

START DATE................. FINISH DATE ....

☆☆☆☆☆

PLOT

THOUGHTS

QUOTES

Book Review

TITLE ....

AUTHOR ....

SERIES ....

SERIES BOOK # .... PAGE COUNT ....

GENRE ....

FORMAT ....

START DATE .... FINISH DATE ....

☆☆☆☆☆

PLOT

THOUGHTS

QUOTES

Book Review

TITLE ....

AUTHOR ....

SERIES...

SERIES BOOK #............... PAGE COUNT...............

GENRE...

FORMAT..

START DATE.................. FINISH DATE ....

☆☆☆☆☆

PLOT

THOUGHTS

QUOTES

Book Review

TITLE ....

AUTHOR ....

SERIES...

SERIES BOOK #............... PAGE COUNT................

GENRE...

FORMAT...

START DATE................. FINISH DATE ....

☆☆☆☆☆

PLOT

_____

THOUGHTS

_____

QUOTES

Book Review

TITLE ....

AUTHOR ....

SERIES...

SERIES BOOK #.............. PAGE COUNT..............

GENRE..

FORMAT...

START DATE................. FINISH DATE ....

☆☆☆☆☆

PLOT

THOUGHTS

QUOTES

Book Review

TITLE ....

AUTHOR ....

SERIES...

SERIES BOOK # .... PAGE COUNT...............

GENRE...

FORMAT...

START DATE................. FINISH DATE ....

☆☆☆☆☆

PLOT

THOUGHTS

QUOTES

Book Review

TITLE ....

AUTHOR ....

SERIES ....

SERIES BOOK # .... PAGE COUNT ....

GENRE ....

FORMAT ....

START DATE .... FINISH DATE ....

☆ ☆ ☆ ☆ ☆

PLOT

THOUGHTS

QUOTES

Book Review

TITLE ....

AUTHOR ....

SERIES ....

SERIES BOOK # .... PAGE COUNT ....

GENRE ....

FORMAT ....

START DATE .... FINISH DATE ....

☆☆☆☆☆

PLOT

_____

THOUGHTS

_____

QUOTES

Book Review

TITLE ....

AUTHOR ....

SERIES ....

SERIES BOOK # .... PAGE COUNT ....

GENRE ....

FORMAT ....

START DATE .... FINISH DATE ....

☆ ☆ ☆ ☆ ☆

PLOT

THOUGHTS

QUOTES

Book Review

TITLE ....

AUTHOR ....

SERIES...

SERIES BOOK #............. PAGE COUNT...............

GENRE..

FORMAT..

START DATE................. FINISH DATE ....

☆☆☆☆☆

PLOT

THOUGHTS

QUOTES

Book Review

TITLE ....

AUTHOR ....

SERIES...

SERIES BOOK #.............. PAGE COUNT.................

GENRE..

FORMAT...

START DATE.................. FINISH DATE ....

☆☆☆☆☆

PLOT

THOUGHTS

QUOTES

Book Review

TITLE ....

AUTHOR ....

SERIES ....

SERIES BOOK # .... PAGE COUNT ....

GENRE ....

FORMAT ....

START DATE .... FINISH DATE ....

☆☆☆☆☆

PLOT

THOUGHTS

QUOTES

Book Review

TITLE ....

AUTHOR ....

SERIES...

SERIES BOOK #............... PAGE COUNT...............

GENRE...

FORMAT..

START DATE.................. FINISH DATE ....

☆☆☆☆☆

PLOT

THOUGHTS

QUOTES

Book Review

TITLE ....

AUTHOR ....

SERIES...

SERIES BOOK #............... PAGE COUNT...............

GENRE..

FORMAT..

START DATE................. FINISH DATE ....

☆☆☆☆☆

PLOT

THOUGHTS

QUOTES

Book Review

TITLE ....

AUTHOR ....

SERIES..

SERIES BOOK #.............. PAGE COUNT...............

GENRE...

FORMAT...

START DATE.................. FINISH DATE ....

☆☆☆☆☆

PLOT

THOUGHTS

QUOTES

Book Review

TITLE ....

AUTHOR ....

SERIES..

SERIES BOOK #.............. PAGE COUNT................

GENRE...

FORMAT...

START DATE................. FINISH DATE ....

☆☆☆☆☆

PLOT

THOUGHTS

QUOTES

Book Review

TITLE ....

AUTHOR ....

SERIES ....

SERIES BOOK # .... PAGE COUNT ....

GENRE ....

FORMAT ....

START DATE .... FINISH DATE ....

☆☆☆☆☆

PLOT

_____

THOUGHTS

_____

QUOTES

Book Review

TITLE ....

AUTHOR ....

SERIES...

SERIES BOOK #............... PAGE COUNT...............

GENRE...

FORMAT...

START DATE................ FINISH DATE ....

☆☆☆☆☆

PLOT

THOUGHTS

QUOTES

Book Review

TITLE ....

AUTHOR ....

SERIES..

SERIES BOOK #............ PAGE COUNT................

GENRE..

FORMAT..

START DATE................ FINISH DATE ....

☆☆☆☆☆

PLOT

THOUGHTS

QUOTES

Book Review

TITLE ....

AUTHOR ....

SERIES...

SERIES BOOK #............. PAGE COUNT...............

GENRE...

FORMAT..

START DATE................. FINISH DATE ....

☆☆☆☆☆

PLOT

THOUGHTS

QUOTES

Book Review

TITLE ....

AUTHOR ....

SERIES..

SERIES BOOK #............. PAGE COUNT................

GENRE..

FORMAT..

START DATE................. FINISH DATE ....

☆☆☆☆☆

PLOT

THOUGHTS

QUOTES

Book Review

TITLE ....

AUTHOR ....

SERIES..

SERIES BOOK #............. PAGE COUNT...............

GENRE..

FORMAT...

START DATE.................. FINISH DATE ....

☆☆☆☆☆

PLOT

THOUGHTS

QUOTES

Book Review

TITLE ....

AUTHOR ....

SERIES..

SERIES BOOK #.............. PAGE COUNT................

GENRE..

FORMAT...

START DATE................. FINISH DATE ....

☆☆☆☆☆

PLOT

_____

THOUGHTS

_____

QUOTES

Book Review

TITLE ....

AUTHOR ....

SERIES ....

SERIES BOOK # .... PAGE COUNT ....

GENRE ....

FORMAT ....

START DATE .... FINISH DATE ....

☆☆☆☆☆

PLOT

THOUGHTS

QUOTES

Book Review

TITLE ....

AUTHOR ....

SERIES..

SERIES BOOK #.............. PAGE COUNT................

GENRE...

FORMAT...

START DATE.................. FINISH DATE ....

☆☆☆☆☆

PLOT

THOUGHTS

QUOTES

Book Review

TITLE ....

AUTHOR ....

SERIES..

SERIES BOOK #.............. PAGE COUNT...............

GENRE..

FORMAT..

START DATE.............. FINISH DATE ....

☆ ☆ ☆ ☆ ☆

PLOT

THOUGHTS

QUOTES

Book Review

TITLE ....

AUTHOR ....

SERIES...

SERIES BOOK #............. PAGE COUNT................

GENRE...

FORMAT...

START DATE................. FINISH DATE ....

☆☆☆☆☆

PLOT

THOUGHTS

QUOTES

Book Review

TITLE ....

AUTHOR ....

SERIES ....

SERIES BOOK # .... PAGE COUNT ....

GENRE ....

FORMAT ....

START DATE .... FINISH DATE ....

☆☆☆☆☆

PLOT

THOUGHTS

QUOTES

Book Review

TITLE ....

AUTHOR ....

SERIES ....

SERIES BOOK # .... PAGE COUNT ....

GENRE ....

FORMAT ....

START DATE .... FINISH DATE ....

☆☆☆☆☆

PLOT

THOUGHTS

QUOTES

Book Review

TITLE ....

AUTHOR ....

SERIES ....

SERIES BOOK # .... PAGE COUNT ....

GENRE ....

FORMAT ....

START DATE .... FINISH DATE ....

☆☆☆☆☆

PLOT

THOUGHTS

QUOTES

Book Review

TITLE ....

AUTHOR ....

SERIES ....

SERIES BOOK # .... PAGE COUNT ....

GENRE ....

FORMAT ....

START DATE .... FINISH DATE ....

☆ ☆ ☆ ☆ ☆

PLOT

THOUGHTS

QUOTES

Book Review

TITLE ....

AUTHOR ....

SERIES ....

SERIES BOOK # .... PAGE COUNT ....

GENRE ....

FORMAT ....

START DATE .... FINISH DATE ....

☆☆☆☆☆

PLOT

THOUGHTS

QUOTES

Book Review

TITLE ....

AUTHOR ....

SERIES..

SERIES BOOK #.............. PAGE COUNT................

GENRE..

FORMAT...

START DATE................ FINISH DATE ....

☆☆☆☆☆

PLOT

THOUGHTS

QUOTES

Book Review

TITLE ....

AUTHOR ....

SERIES ....

SERIES BOOK # .... PAGE COUNT ....

GENRE ....

FORMAT ....

START DATE .... FINISH DATE ....

☆☆☆☆☆

PLOT

THOUGHTS

QUOTES

Book Review

TITLE ....

AUTHOR ....

SERIES...

SERIES BOOK #............. PAGE COUNT..............

GENRE...

FORMAT...

START DATE................. FINISH DATE ....

☆ ☆ ☆ ☆ ☆

PLOT

THOUGHTS

QUOTES

Book Review

TITLE ....

AUTHOR ....

SERIES ....

SERIES BOOK # .... PAGE COUNT ....

GENRE ....

FORMAT ....

START DATE .... FINISH DATE ....

☆☆☆☆☆

PLOT

THOUGHTS

QUOTES

Book Review

TITLE ....

AUTHOR ....

SERIES..

SERIES BOOK #............... PAGE COUNT...............

GENRE...

FORMAT..

START DATE................. FINISH DATE ....

☆☆☆☆☆

PLOT

THOUGHTS

QUOTES

Book Review

TITLE ....

AUTHOR ....

SERIES...

SERIES BOOK # .... PAGE COUNT................

GENRE..

FORMAT...

START DATE................. FINISH DATE ....

☆☆☆☆☆

PLOT

THOUGHTS

QUOTES

Book Review

TITLE ....

AUTHOR ....

SERIES...

SERIES BOOK #.............. PAGE COUNT...............

GENRE..

FORMAT...

START DATE................. FINISH DATE ....

☆☆☆☆☆

PLOT

THOUGHTS

QUOTES

Book Review

TITLE ....

AUTHOR ....

SERIES ....

SERIES BOOK # .... PAGE COUNT ....

GENRE ....

FORMAT ....

START DATE .... FINISH DATE ....

☆☆☆☆☆

PLOT

THOUGHTS

QUOTES

Book Review

TITLE ....

AUTHOR ....

SERIES...

SERIES BOOK #................ PAGE COUNT..............

GENRE..

FORMAT...

START DATE................. FINISH DATE ....

☆☆☆☆☆

PLOT

THOUGHTS

QUOTES

Book Review

TITLE ....

AUTHOR ....

SERIES ....

SERIES BOOK # .... PAGE COUNT ....

GENRE ....

FORMAT ....

START DATE .... FINISH DATE ....

☆☆☆☆☆

PLOT

THOUGHTS

QUOTES

Book Review

TITLE ....

AUTHOR ....

SERIES...

SERIES BOOK #................ PAGE COUNT................

GENRE..

FORMAT...

START DATE................. FINISH DATE ....

☆☆☆☆☆

PLOT

THOUGHTS

QUOTES

Book Review

TITLE ....

AUTHOR ....

SERIES...

SERIES BOOK #................ PAGE COUNT................

GENRE...

FORMAT...

START DATE.................. FINISH DATE ....

☆☆☆☆☆

PLOT

THOUGHTS

QUOTES

Book Review

TITLE ....

AUTHOR ....

SERIES..

SERIES BOOK #.............. PAGE COUNT................

GENRE...

FORMAT..

START DATE................. FINISH DATE ....

☆☆☆☆☆

PLOT

THOUGHTS

QUOTES

Book Review

TITLE ....
AUTHOR ....
SERIES ....
SERIES BOOK # .... PAGE COUNT ....
GENRE ....
FORMAT ....
START DATE .... FINISH DATE ....

☆☆☆☆☆

PLOT

THOUGHTS

QUOTES

Book Review

TITLE ....

AUTHOR ....

SERIES...

SERIES BOOK #................ PAGE COUNT...............

GENRE...

FORMAT...

START DATE................. FINISH DATE ....

☆☆☆☆☆

PLOT

THOUGHTS

QUOTES

Book Review

TITLE ....

AUTHOR ....

SERIES...

SERIES BOOK #................ PAGE COUNT...............

GENRE...

FORMAT...

START DATE.................. FINISH DATE ....

☆☆☆☆☆

PLOT

THOUGHTS

QUOTES

Book Review

TITLE ....

AUTHOR ....

SERIES...

SERIES BOOK #................ PAGE COUNT...............

GENRE...

FORMAT..

START DATE................. FINISH DATE ....

☆ ☆ ☆ ☆ ☆

PLOT

THOUGHTS

QUOTES

Book Review

TITLE ....

AUTHOR ....

SERIES..

SERIES BOOK # .... PAGE COUNT...............

GENRE...

FORMAT...

START DATE................. FINISH DATE ....

☆☆☆☆☆

PLOT

THOUGHTS

QUOTES

Book Review

TITLE ....

AUTHOR ....

SERIES ....

SERIES BOOK # .... PAGE COUNT ....

GENRE ....

FORMAT ....

START DATE .... FINISH DATE ....

☆☆☆☆☆

PLOT

_____

THOUGHTS

_____

QUOTES

Book Review

TITLE ....

AUTHOR ....

SERIES...

SERIES BOOK #............... PAGE COUNT................

GENRE...

FORMAT..

START DATE................. FINISH DATE ....

☆☆☆☆☆

PLOT

THOUGHTS

QUOTES

Book Review

TITLE ....

AUTHOR ....

SERIES...

SERIES BOOK #.............. PAGE COUNT................

GENRE..

FORMAT..

START DATE................. FINISH DATE ....

☆☆☆☆☆

PLOT

THOUGHTS

QUOTES

Book Review

TITLE ....

AUTHOR ....

SERIES...

SERIES BOOK #............. PAGE COUNT................

GENRE...

FORMAT..

START DATE................. FINISH DATE ....

☆☆☆☆☆

PLOT

THOUGHTS

QUOTES

Book Review

TITLE ....

AUTHOR ....

SERIES..

SERIES BOOK #............... PAGE COUNT................

GENRE...

FORMAT...

START DATE................... FINISH DATE ....

☆ ☆ ☆ ☆ ☆

PLOT

THOUGHTS

QUOTES

Book Review

TITLE ....

AUTHOR ....

SERIES...

SERIES BOOK #............. PAGE COUNT.................

GENRE..

FORMAT..

START DATE................. FINISH DATE ....

☆ ☆ ☆ ☆ ☆

PLOT

THOUGHTS

QUOTES

Book Review

TITLE ....

AUTHOR ....

SERIES...

SERIES BOOK #............. PAGE COUNT...............

GENRE..

FORMAT...

START DATE.................. FINISH DATE ....

☆☆☆☆☆

PLOT

THOUGHTS

QUOTES

Book Review

TITLE ....

AUTHOR ....

SERIES ....

SERIES BOOK # .... PAGE COUNT ....

GENRE ....

FORMAT ....

START DATE .... FINISH DATE ....

☆☆☆☆☆

PLOT

THOUGHTS

QUOTES

Book Review

TITLE ....

AUTHOR ....

SERIES...

SERIES BOOK #.............. PAGE COUNT...............

GENRE..

FORMAT...

START DATE.................. FINISH DATE ....

☆☆☆☆☆

PLOT

THOUGHTS

QUOTES

Book Review

TITLE ....

AUTHOR ....

SERIES...

SERIES BOOK #.................. PAGE COUNT...............

GENRE..

FORMAT..

START DATE.................. FINISH DATE ....

☆☆☆☆☆

PLOT

THOUGHTS

QUOTES

Book Review

TITLE ....

AUTHOR ....

SERIES..

SERIES BOOK #................ PAGE COUNT................

GENRE...

FORMAT...

START DATE................. FINISH DATE ....

☆☆☆☆☆

PLOT

THOUGHTS

QUOTES

Book Review

TITLE ....

AUTHOR ....

SERIES ....

SERIES BOOK # .... PAGE COUNT ....

GENRE ....

FORMAT ....

START DATE .... FINISH DATE ....

☆☆☆☆☆

PLOT

THOUGHTS

QUOTES

Book Review

TITLE ....

AUTHOR ....

SERIES...

SERIES BOOK #............ PAGE COUNT...............

GENRE...

FORMAT...

START DATE................. FINISH DATE ....

☆☆☆☆☆

PLOT

THOUGHTS

QUOTES

Book Review

TITLE ....
AUTHOR ....
SERIES ....
SERIES BOOK # .... PAGE COUNT ....
GENRE ....
FORMAT ....
START DATE .... FINISH DATE ....

☆☆☆☆☆

PLOT

THOUGHTS

QUOTES

Book Review

TITLE ....

AUTHOR ....

SERIES...

SERIES BOOK # .... PAGE COUNT ....

GENRE ....

FORMAT..

START DATE .... FINISH DATE ....

☆☆☆☆☆

PLOT

___

THOUGHTS

___

QUOTES

Book Review

TITLE ....

AUTHOR ....

SERIES..

SERIES BOOK #............. PAGE COUNT..............

GENRE...

FORMAT..

START DATE.............. FINISH DATE ....

☆☆☆☆☆

PLOT

THOUGHTS

QUOTES

Book Review

TITLE ....

AUTHOR ....

SERIES..

SERIES BOOK #................ PAGE COUNT.................

GENRE..

FORMAT...

START DATE................. FINISH DATE ....

☆☆☆☆☆

PLOT

THOUGHTS

QUOTES

Book Review

TITLE ....

AUTHOR ....

SERIES ....

SERIES BOOK # .... PAGE COUNT................

GENRE ....

FORMAT ....

START DATE................. FINISH DATE ....

PLOT

THOUGHTS

QUOTES

Book Review

TITLE ....

AUTHOR ....

SERIES ....

SERIES BOOK # .... PAGE COUNT ....

GENRE ....

FORMAT ....

START DATE .... FINISH DATE ....

☆☆☆☆☆

PLOT

THOUGHTS

QUOTES

Book Review

TITLE ....

AUTHOR ....

SERIES...

SERIES BOOK #.............. PAGE COUNT..............

GENRE...

FORMAT...

START DATE.............. FINISH DATE ....

PLOT

THOUGHTS

QUOTES

Book Review

TITLE ....

AUTHOR ....

SERIES...

SERIES BOOK #............. PAGE COUNT...............

GENRE..

FORMAT..

START DATE................. FINISH DATE ....

☆☆☆☆☆

PLOT

THOUGHTS

QUOTES

Book Review

TITLE ....
AUTHOR ....
SERIES ....
SERIES BOOK # .... PAGE COUNT ....
GENRE ....
FORMAT ....
START DATE .... FINISH DATE ....

☆☆☆☆☆

PLOT

THOUGHTS

QUOTES

Book Review

TITLE ....
AUTHOR ....
SERIES...
SERIES BOOK #.............. PAGE COUNT..............
GENRE..
FORMAT..
START DATE............... FINISH DATE ....

☆☆☆☆☆

PLOT

THOUGHTS

QUOTES

Book Review

TITLE ....

AUTHOR ....

SERIES ....

SERIES BOOK # .... PAGE COUNT ....

GENRE ....

FORMAT ....

START DATE .... FINISH DATE ....

☆☆☆☆☆

PLOT

THOUGHTS

QUOTES

Book Review

TITLE ....

AUTHOR ....

SERIES...

SERIES BOOK #............. PAGE COUNT...............

GENRE...

FORMAT...

START DATE................. FINISH DATE ....

☆☆☆☆☆

PLOT

THOUGHTS

QUOTES

Book Review

TITLE ....

AUTHOR ....

SERIES ....

SERIES BOOK # .... PAGE COUNT ....

GENRE ....

FORMAT ....

START DATE .... FINISH DATE ....

☆☆☆☆☆

PLOT

THOUGHTS

QUOTES

Book Review

TITLE ....

AUTHOR ....

SERIES ....

SERIES BOOK # .... PAGE COUNT ....

GENRE ....

FORMAT ....

START DATE .... FINISH DATE ....

☆☆☆☆☆

PLOT

THOUGHTS

QUOTES

Book Review

TITLE ....

AUTHOR ....

SERIES..

SERIES BOOK #................ PAGE COUNT................

GENRE..

FORMAT..

START DATE................ FINISH DATE ....

☆ ☆ ☆ ☆ ☆

PLOT

_____

THOUGHTS

_____

QUOTES

Book Review

TITLE ....

AUTHOR ....

SERIES..

SERIES BOOK #.............. PAGE COUNT...............

GENRE...

FORMAT..

START DATE................ FINISH DATE ....

☆☆☆☆☆

PLOT

THOUGHTS

QUOTES

Book Review

TITLE ....

AUTHOR ....

SERIES ....

SERIES BOOK # .... PAGE COUNT ....

GENRE ....

FORMAT ....

START DATE .... FINISH DATE ....

☆☆☆☆☆

PLOT

THOUGHTS

QUOTES

Book Review

TITLE ....

AUTHOR ....

SERIES...

SERIES BOOK #.............. PAGE COUNT...............

GENRE...

FORMAT...

START DATE.................. FINISH DATE ....

PLOT

THOUGHTS

QUOTES

Book Review

TITLE ....

AUTHOR ....

SERIES ....

SERIES BOOK # .... PAGE COUNT.................

GENRE ....

FORMAT...

START DATE.................. FINISH DATE ....

☆☆☆☆☆

PLOT

THOUGHTS

QUOTES

Book Review

TITLE ....

AUTHOR ....

SERIES...

SERIES BOOK #............... PAGE COUNT...............

GENRE...

FORMAT...

START DATE................. FINISH DATE ....

☆☆☆☆☆

PLOT

THOUGHTS

QUOTES

Book Review

TITLE ....

AUTHOR ....

SERIES...

SERIES BOOK #.............. PAGE COUNT................

GENRE...

FORMAT..

START DATE.................. FINISH DATE ....

☆☆☆☆☆

PLOT

THOUGHTS

QUOTES

Book Review

TITLE ....

AUTHOR ....

SERIES..

SERIES BOOK #............. PAGE COUNT...............

GENRE...

FORMAT..

START DATE................. FINISH DATE ....

☆☆☆☆☆

PLOT

THOUGHTS

QUOTES

Book Review

TITLE ....

AUTHOR ....

SERIES ....

SERIES BOOK # .... PAGE COUNT ....

GENRE ....

FORMAT ....

START DATE .... FINISH DATE ....

☆☆☆☆☆

PLOT

THOUGHTS

QUOTES

Book Review

TITLE ....

AUTHOR ....

SERIES...

SERIES BOOK #............. PAGE COUNT.............

GENRE...

FORMAT...

START DATE................ FINISH DATE ....

☆☆☆☆☆

PLOT

THOUGHTS

QUOTES

Book Review

TITLE ....

AUTHOR ....

SERIES..

SERIES BOOK #.............. PAGE COUNT..............

GENRE..

FORMAT..

START DATE................. FINISH DATE ....

☆☆☆☆☆

PLOT

THOUGHTS

QUOTES

Book Review

TITLE ....

AUTHOR ....

SERIES...

SERIES BOOK #.............. PAGE COUNT..............

GENRE...

FORMAT..

START DATE................. FINISH DATE ....

☆☆☆☆☆

PLOT

THOUGHTS

QUOTES

Book Review

TITLE ....
AUTHOR ....
SERIES..
SERIES BOOK #.............. PAGE COUNT.................
GENRE...
FORMAT..
START DATE.................. FINISH DATE ....

☆☆☆☆☆

PLOT

THOUGHTS

QUOTES

Book Review

TITLE ....

AUTHOR ....

SERIES..

SERIES BOOK #............. PAGE COUNT...............

GENRE..

FORMAT..

START DATE................. FINISH DATE ....

☆☆☆☆☆

PLOT

THOUGHTS

QUOTES

Book Review

TITLE ....

AUTHOR ....

SERIES ....

SERIES BOOK # .... PAGE COUNT ....

GENRE ....

FORMAT ....

START DATE .... FINISH DATE ....

☆☆☆☆☆

PLOT

THOUGHTS

QUOTES

Book Review

TITLE ....

AUTHOR ....

SERIES...

SERIES BOOK #.............. PAGE COUNT..................

GENRE...

FORMAT...

START DATE................. FINISH DATE ....

☆☆☆☆☆

PLOT

THOUGHTS

QUOTES

Book Review

TITLE ....

AUTHOR ....

SERIES..

SERIES BOOK #................ PAGE COUNT...............

GENRE...

FORMAT...

START DATE................. FINISH DATE ....

☆☆☆☆☆

PLOT

THOUGHTS

QUOTES

Book Review

TITLE ....

AUTHOR ....

SERIES...

SERIES BOOK #............. PAGE COUNT...............

GENRE...

FORMAT...

START DATE................ FINISH DATE ....

☆☆☆☆☆

PLOT

THOUGHTS

QUOTES

Book Review

TITLE ....

AUTHOR ....

SERIES ....

SERIES BOOK # .... PAGE COUNT ....

GENRE ....

FORMAT ....

START DATE .... FINISH DATE ....

☆☆☆☆☆

PLOT

THOUGHTS

QUOTES

Book Review

TITLE ....

AUTHOR ....

SERIES..

SERIES BOOK #............. PAGE COUNT................

GENRE...

FORMAT...

START DATE................. FINISH DATE ....

☆☆☆☆☆

PLOT

THOUGHTS

QUOTES

Book Review

TITLE ....

AUTHOR ....

SERIES..

SERIES BOOK #............... PAGE COUNT...............

GENRE..

FORMAT..

START DATE................. FINISH DATE ....

☆☆☆☆☆

PLOT

THOUGHTS

QUOTES

Book Review

TITLE ....

AUTHOR ....

SERIES...

SERIES BOOK #.............. PAGE COUNT...............

GENRE..

FORMAT...

START DATE................. FINISH DATE ....

☆☆☆☆☆

PLOT

THOUGHTS

QUOTES

Book Review

TITLE ....

AUTHOR ....

SERIES...

SERIES BOOK #............ PAGE COUNT............

GENRE..

FORMAT..

START DATE................ FINISH DATE ....

☆☆☆☆☆

PLOT

THOUGHTS

QUOTES

Book Review

TITLE ....

AUTHOR ....

SERIES...

SERIES BOOK #............. PAGE COUNT.................

GENRE...

FORMAT...

START DATE................ FINISH DATE ....

☆☆☆☆☆

PLOT

THOUGHTS

QUOTES

Book Review

TITLE ....

AUTHOR ....

SERIES...

SERIES BOOK # .... PAGE COUNT...................

GENRE..

FORMAT...

START DATE.................... FINISH DATE ....

☆ ☆ ☆ ☆ ☆

PLOT

THOUGHTS

QUOTES

Book Review

TITLE ....

AUTHOR ....

SERIES...

SERIES BOOK #............. PAGE COUNT..............

GENRE...

FORMAT...

START DATE................. FINISH DATE ....

☆☆☆☆☆

PLOT

THOUGHTS

QUOTES

Book Review

TITLE ....

AUTHOR ....

SERIES...

SERIES BOOK #............. PAGE COUNT................

GENRE..

FORMAT...

START DATE.................. FINISH DATE ....

☆☆☆☆☆

PLOT

THOUGHTS

QUOTES

Book Review

TITLE ....

AUTHOR ....

SERIES..

SERIES BOOK #.............. PAGE COUNT...............

GENRE..

FORMAT..

START DATE.............. FINISH DATE ....

☆☆☆☆☆

PLOT

THOUGHTS

QUOTES

Book Review

TITLE ....

AUTHOR ....

SERIES ....

SERIES BOOK # .... PAGE COUNT ....

GENRE ....

FORMAT ....

START DATE .... FINISH DATE ....

PLOT

THOUGHTS

QUOTES

Book Review

TITLE ....

AUTHOR ....

SERIES...

SERIES BOOK #............... PAGE COUNT...............

GENRE...

FORMAT...

START DATE.................. FINISH DATE ....

☆☆☆☆☆

PLOT

THOUGHTS

QUOTES

Book Review

TITLE ....

AUTHOR ....

SERIES ....

SERIES BOOK # .... PAGE COUNT ....

GENRE ....

FORMAT ....

START DATE .... FINISH DATE ....

☆☆☆☆☆

PLOT

THOUGHTS

QUOTES

Book Review

TITLE ....

AUTHOR ....

SERIES...

SERIES BOOK #.............. PAGE COUNT..............

GENRE..

FORMAT...

START DATE................ FINISH DATE ....

☆☆☆☆☆

PLOT

_____

THOUGHTS

_____

QUOTES

Book Review

TITLE ....

AUTHOR ....

SERIES..

SERIES BOOK #.................. PAGE COUNT..................

GENRE..

FORMAT..

START DATE.................. FINISH DATE ....

☆ ☆ ☆ ☆ ☆

PLOT

THOUGHTS

QUOTES

Book Review

TITLE ....

AUTHOR ....

SERIES..

SERIES BOOK #................ PAGE COUNT................

GENRE..

FORMAT...

START DATE................... FINISH DATE ....

☆☆☆☆☆

PLOT

THOUGHTS

QUOTES

Book Review

TITLE ....

AUTHOR ....

SERIES ....

SERIES BOOK # .... PAGE COUNT ....

GENRE ....

FORMAT ....

START DATE .... FINISH DATE ....

☆☆☆☆☆

PLOT

THOUGHTS

QUOTES

Book Review

TITLE ....

AUTHOR ....

SERIES...

SERIES BOOK #................ PAGE COUNT.................

GENRE ....

FORMAT..

START DATE.................. FINISH DATE ....

☆☆☆☆☆

PLOT

THOUGHTS

QUOTES

Book Review

TITLE ....

AUTHOR ....

SERIES ....

SERIES BOOK # .... PAGE COUNT ....

GENRE ....

FORMAT ....

START DATE .... FINISH DATE ....

☆☆☆☆☆

PLOT

THOUGHTS

QUOTES

Book Review

TITLE ....

AUTHOR ....

SERIES ....

SERIES BOOK # .... PAGE COUNT ....

GENRE ....

FORMAT ....

START DATE .... FINISH DATE ....

☆☆☆☆☆

PLOT

THOUGHTS

QUOTES

Book Review

TITLE ....

AUTHOR ....

SERIES..

SERIES BOOK #.................. PAGE COUNT................

GENRE...

FORMAT..

START DATE................... FINISH DATE ....

☆☆☆☆☆

PLOT

_____

THOUGHTS

_____

QUOTES

Book Review

TITLE ....

AUTHOR ....

SERIES...

SERIES BOOK #.............. PAGE COUNT...............

GENRE...

FORMAT..

START DATE................. FINISH DATE ....

☆☆☆☆☆

PLOT

THOUGHTS

QUOTES

Book Review

TITLE ....

AUTHOR ....

SERIES..

SERIES BOOK #................. PAGE COUNT.................

GENRE..

FORMAT..

START DATE................. FINISH DATE ....

☆☆☆☆☆

PLOT

THOUGHTS

QUOTES

Book Review

TITLE ....

AUTHOR ....

SERIES ....

SERIES BOOK # .... PAGE COUNT ....

GENRE ....

FORMAT ....

START DATE .... FINISH DATE ....

☆☆☆☆☆

PLOT

THOUGHTS

QUOTES

Book Review

TITLE ....

AUTHOR ....

SERIES ....

SERIES BOOK # .... PAGE COUNT ....

GENRE ....

FORMAT ....

START DATE .... FINISH DATE ....

☆☆☆☆☆

PLOT

THOUGHTS

QUOTES

Book Review

TITLE ....

AUTHOR ....

SERIES...

SERIES BOOK #............. PAGE COUNT.................

GENRE..

FORMAT..

START DATE................. FINISH DATE ....

☆☆☆☆☆

PLOT

THOUGHTS

QUOTES

Book Review

TITLE ....

AUTHOR ....

SERIES..

SERIES BOOK # .... PAGE COUNT...............

GENRE...

FORMAT...

START DATE................. FINISH DATE ....

☆☆☆☆☆

PLOT

THOUGHTS

QUOTES

Book Review

TITLE ....

AUTHOR ....

SERIES...

SERIES BOOK #............ PAGE COUNT................

GENRE...

FORMAT..

START DATE................ FINISH DATE ....

☆☆☆☆☆

PLOT

THOUGHTS

QUOTES

Book Review

TITLE ....

AUTHOR ....

SERIES ....

SERIES BOOK # .... PAGE COUNT ....

GENRE ....

FORMAT ....

START DATE .... FINISH DATE ....

☆ ☆ ☆ ☆ ☆

PLOT

THOUGHTS

QUOTES

Book Review

TITLE ....

AUTHOR ....

SERIES ....

SERIES BOOK # .... PAGE COUNT ....

GENRE ....

FORMAT ....

START DATE .... FINISH DATE ....

☆☆☆☆☆

PLOT

THOUGHTS

QUOTES

Book Review

TITLE ....

AUTHOR ....

SERIES...

SERIES BOOK #................ PAGE COUNT................

GENRE...

FORMAT...

START DATE................. FINISH DATE ....

☆☆☆☆☆

PLOT

THOUGHTS

QUOTES

Book Review

TITLE ....

AUTHOR ....

SERIES...

SERIES BOOK #............... PAGE COUNT...............

GENRE...

FORMAT...

 START DATE................. FINISH DATE ....

☆☆☆☆☆

PLOT

THOUGHTS

QUOTES

Book Review

TITLE ....

AUTHOR ....

SERIES ....

SERIES BOOK # .... PAGE COUNT ....

GENRE ....

FORMAT ....

START DATE .... FINISH DATE ....

PLOT

THOUGHTS

QUOTES

Book Review

TITLE ....

AUTHOR ....

SERIES..

SERIES BOOK #............... PAGE COUNT..................

GENRE..

FORMAT...

START DATE................ FINISH DATE ....

☆☆☆☆☆

PLOT

THOUGHTS

QUOTES

Book Review

TITLE ....

AUTHOR ....

SERIES..

SERIES BOOK #................ PAGE COUNT...............

GENRE..

FORMAT...

START DATE.................. FINISH DATE ....

☆ ☆ ☆ ☆ ☆

PLOT

THOUGHTS

QUOTES

Book Review

TITLE ....

AUTHOR ....

SERIES ....

SERIES BOOK # .... PAGE COUNT ....

GENRE ....

FORMAT ....

START DATE .... FINISH DATE ....

☆☆☆☆☆

PLOT

THOUGHTS

QUOTES

Book Review

TITLE ....

AUTHOR ....

SERIES...

SERIES BOOK #.................. PAGE COUNT................

GENRE...

FORMAT...

START DATE.................. FINISH DATE ....

☆ ☆ ☆ ☆ ☆

PLOT
_____

THOUGHTS
_____

QUOTES

Book Review

TITLE ....

AUTHOR ....

SERIES...

SERIES BOOK #................ PAGE COUNT.................

GENRE...

FORMAT...

START DATE................. FINISH DATE ....

☆☆☆☆☆

PLOT

THOUGHTS

QUOTES

Book Review

TITLE ....

AUTHOR ....

SERIES ....

SERIES BOOK # .... PAGE COUNT ....

GENRE ....

FORMAT ....

START DATE .... FINISH DATE ....

☆☆☆☆☆

PLOT

THOUGHTS

QUOTES

Book Review

TITLE ....

AUTHOR ....

SERIES...

SERIES BOOK #.............. PAGE COUNT..............

GENRE...

FORMAT...

START DATE.................. FINISH DATE ....

☆☆☆☆☆

PLOT

THOUGHTS

QUOTES

Book Review

TITLE ....

AUTHOR ....

SERIES...

SERIES BOOK #............. PAGE COUNT.................

GENRE..

FORMAT...

START DATE................. FINISH DATE ....

☆☆☆☆☆

PLOT

THOUGHTS

QUOTES

Book Review

TITLE ....

AUTHOR ....

SERIES ....

SERIES BOOK # .... PAGE COUNT ....

GENRE ....

FORMAT ....

START DATE .... FINISH DATE ....

☆☆☆☆☆

PLOT

___

THOUGHTS

___

QUOTES

Book Review

TITLE ....

AUTHOR ....

SERIES..

SERIES BOOK #................ PAGE COUNT................

GENRE..

FORMAT..

START DATE................ FINISH DATE ....

☆☆☆☆☆

PLOT

THOUGHTS

QUOTES

Book Review

TITLE ....

AUTHOR ....

SERIES...

SERIES BOOK #.............. PAGE COUNT................

GENRE..

FORMAT...

START DATE.................. FINISH DATE ....

☆☆☆☆☆

PLOT

_____

THOUGHTS

_____

QUOTES

Book Review

TITLE ....

AUTHOR ....

SERIES ....

SERIES BOOK # .... PAGE COUNT ....

GENRE ....

FORMAT ....

START DATE .... FINISH DATE ....

☆☆☆☆☆

PLOT

THOUGHTS

QUOTES

Book Review

TITLE ....

AUTHOR ....

SERIES..

SERIES BOOK #.............. PAGE COUNT................

GENRE..

FORMAT...

START DATE................ FINISH DATE ....

☆☆☆☆☆

PLOT

THOUGHTS

QUOTES

Book Review

TITLE ....

AUTHOR ....

SERIES ....

SERIES BOOK # .... PAGE COUNT ....

GENRE ....

FORMAT ....

START DATE .... FINISH DATE ....

PLOT

THOUGHTS

QUOTES

Book Review

TITLE ....

AUTHOR ....

SERIES...

SERIES BOOK #................ PAGE COUNT..............

GENRE..

FORMAT..

START DATE................. FINISH DATE ....

☆☆☆☆☆

PLOT

THOUGHTS

QUOTES

Book Review

TITLE ....

AUTHOR ....

SERIES ....

SERIES BOOK # .... PAGE COUNT ....

GENRE ....

FORMAT ....

START DATE .... FINISH DATE ....

☆☆☆☆☆

PLOT

THOUGHTS

QUOTES

Book Review

TITLE ....

AUTHOR ....

SERIES..

SERIES BOOK #.............. PAGE COUNT................

GENRE..

FORMAT..

START DATE................ FINISH DATE ....

☆☆☆☆☆

PLOT

THOUGHTS

QUOTES

Book Review

TITLE ....

AUTHOR ....

SERIES ....

SERIES BOOK # .... PAGE COUNT.............

GENRE ....

FORMAT ....

START DATE .... FINISH DATE ....

☆☆☆☆☆

PLOT

THOUGHTS

QUOTES

Book Review

TITLE ....

AUTHOR ....

SERIES..

SERIES BOOK #............. PAGE COUNT...............

GENRE...

FORMAT...

START DATE................. FINISH DATE ....

PLOT

THOUGHTS

QUOTES

Book Review

TITLE ....

AUTHOR ....

SERIES..

SERIES BOOK #............. PAGE COUNT................

GENRE ....

FORMAT..

START DATE.................. FINISH DATE ....

☆☆☆☆☆

PLOT

THOUGHTS

QUOTES

Book Review

TITLE ....

AUTHOR ....

SERIES...

SERIES BOOK #.............. PAGE COUNT...............

GENRE..

FORMAT...

START DATE.................. FINISH DATE ....

☆☆☆☆☆

PLOT

THOUGHTS

QUOTES

Book Review

TITLE ....

AUTHOR ....

SERIES ....

SERIES BOOK # .... PAGE COUNT ....

GENRE ....

FORMAT ....

START DATE .... FINISH DATE ....

☆☆☆☆☆

PLOT

THOUGHTS

QUOTES

Book Review

TITLE ....

AUTHOR ....

SERIES..

SERIES BOOK #................ PAGE COUNT................

GENRE...

FORMAT...

START DATE................ FINISH DATE ....

☆☆☆☆☆

PLOT

THOUGHTS

QUOTES

Book Review

TITLE ....

AUTHOR ....

SERIES ....

SERIES BOOK # .... PAGE COUNT ....

GENRE ....

FORMAT ....

START DATE .... FINISH DATE ....

☆☆☆☆☆

PLOT

THOUGHTS

QUOTES

Book Review

TITLE ....

AUTHOR ....

SERIES ....

SERIES BOOK # .... PAGE COUNT...............

GENRE ....

FORMAT ....

START DATE .... FINISH DATE ....

☆☆☆☆☆

PLOT

THOUGHTS

QUOTES

Book Review

TITLE ....

AUTHOR ....

SERIES...

SERIES BOOK #............. PAGE COUNT...............

GENRE..

FORMAT..

START DATE.................. FINISH DATE ....

☆☆☆☆☆

PLOT

THOUGHTS

QUOTES

Book Review

TITLE ....

AUTHOR ....

SERIES...

SERIES BOOK #............... PAGE COUNT...............

GENRE..

FORMAT...

START DATE................. FINISH DATE ....

☆☆☆☆☆

PLOT

THOUGHTS

QUOTES

Book Review

TITLE ....

AUTHOR ....

SERIES..

SERIES BOOK #................ PAGE COUNT................

GENRE...

FORMAT..

START DATE.................. FINISH DATE ....

★★★★★

PLOT

THOUGHTS

QUOTES

Book Review

TITLE ....

AUTHOR ....

SERIES..

SERIES BOOK #.............. PAGE COUNT.................

GENRE...

FORMAT..

START DATE................. FINISH DATE ....

☆☆☆☆☆

PLOT

THOUGHTS

QUOTES

Book Review

TITLE ....

AUTHOR ....

SERIES ....

SERIES BOOK # .... PAGE COUNT ....

GENRE ....

FORMAT ....

START DATE .... FINISH DATE ....

☆ ☆ ☆ ☆ ☆

PLOT

THOUGHTS

QUOTES

Book Review

TITLE ....

AUTHOR ....

SERIES...

SERIES BOOK #............... PAGE COUNT..............

GENRE..

FORMAT..

START DATE.................. FINISH DATE ....

☆☆☆☆☆

PLOT

THOUGHTS

QUOTES

Book Review

TITLE ....

AUTHOR ....

SERIES ....

SERIES BOOK # .... PAGE COUNT ....

GENRE ....

FORMAT ....

START DATE .... FINISH DATE ....

☆ ☆ ☆ ☆ ☆

PLOT

THOUGHTS

QUOTES

Book Review

TITLE ....

AUTHOR ....

SERIES..

SERIES BOOK #.............. PAGE COUNT...............

GENRE..

FORMAT..

START DATE................. FINISH DATE ....

☆☆☆☆☆

PLOT

THOUGHTS

QUOTES

Book Review

TITLE ....

AUTHOR ....

SERIES ....

SERIES BOOK #.................. PAGE COUNT...................

GENRE ....

FORMAT..

START DATE.................. FINISH DATE ....

☆☆☆☆☆

PLOT

THOUGHTS

QUOTES

Book Review

TITLE ....

AUTHOR ....

SERIES...

SERIES BOOK #............ PAGE COUNT...............

GENRE..

FORMAT..

START DATE.................. FINISH DATE ....

☆☆☆☆☆

PLOT

THOUGHTS

QUOTES

Book Review

TITLE ....

AUTHOR ....

SERIES..

SERIES BOOK #............... PAGE COUNT...............

GENRE..

FORMAT..

START DATE................. FINISH DATE ....

☆☆☆☆☆

PLOT

THOUGHTS

QUOTES

Book Review

TITLE ....

AUTHOR ....

SERIES...

SERIES BOOK #.............. PAGE COUNT..................

GENRE..

FORMAT...

START DATE.................. FINISH DATE ....

☆☆☆☆☆

PLOT

THOUGHTS

QUOTES

Book Review

TITLE ....

AUTHOR ....

SERIES ....

SERIES BOOK # .... PAGE COUNT ....

GENRE ....

FORMAT ....

START DATE .... FINISH DATE ....

☆☆☆☆☆

PLOT

THOUGHTS

QUOTES

Book Review

TITLE ....

AUTHOR ....

SERIES ....

SERIES BOOK # .... PAGE COUNT ....

GENRE ....

FORMAT ....

START DATE .... FINISH DATE ....

☆☆☆☆☆

PLOT

THOUGHTS

QUOTES

Book Review

TITLE ....

AUTHOR ....

SERIES ....

SERIES BOOK # .... PAGE COUNT ....

GENRE ....

FORMAT ....

START DATE .... FINISH DATE ....

☆☆☆☆☆

PLOT

THOUGHTS

QUOTES

Book Review

TITLE ....

AUTHOR ....

SERIES...

SERIES BOOK #............ PAGE COUNT...........

GENRE...

FORMAT...

START DATE.............. FINISH DATE ....

☆☆☆☆☆

PLOT

THOUGHTS

QUOTES

Book Review

TITLE ....

AUTHOR ....

SERIES...

SERIES BOOK #............. PAGE COUNT..............

GENRE..

FORMAT...

START DATE................. FINISH DATE ....

☆☆☆☆☆

PLOT

THOUGHTS

QUOTES

Book Review

TITLE ....

AUTHOR ....

SERIES...

SERIES BOOK #............. PAGE COUNT................

GENRE...

FORMAT...

START DATE................. FINISH DATE ....

☆☆☆☆☆

PLOT

THOUGHTS

QUOTES

Book Review

TITLE ....

AUTHOR ....

SERIES ....

SERIES BOOK # .... PAGE COUNT...............

GENRE ....

FORMAT ....

START DATE................. FINISH DATE ....

☆☆☆☆☆

PLOT

THOUGHTS

QUOTES

Book Review

TITLE ....

AUTHOR ....

SERIES...

SERIES BOOK #.............. PAGE COUNT................

GENRE...

FORMAT...

START DATE................. FINISH DATE ....

☆☆☆☆☆

PLOT

THOUGHTS

QUOTES

Book Review

TITLE ....

AUTHOR ....

SERIES...

SERIES BOOK # .... PAGE COUNT.................

GENRE..

FORMAT..

START DATE................. FINISH DATE ....

☆☆☆☆☆

PLOT

THOUGHTS

QUOTES

Book Review

TITLE ....

AUTHOR ....

SERIES...

SERIES BOOK #............... PAGE COUNT.................

GENRE...

FORMAT...

START DATE................. FINISH DATE ....

☆ ☆ ☆ ☆ ☆

PLOT

THOUGHTS

QUOTES

Book Review

TITLE ....

AUTHOR ....

SERIES...

SERIES BOOK #............. PAGE COUNT...............

GENRE...

FORMAT...

START DATE................ FINISH DATE ....

☆☆☆☆☆

PLOT

THOUGHTS

QUOTES

Book Review

TITLE ....

AUTHOR ....

SERIES..

SERIES BOOK #............. PAGE COUNT...............

GENRE..

FORMAT...

START DATE................. FINISH DATE ....

☆☆☆☆☆

PLOT

THOUGHTS

QUOTES

Book Review

TITLE ....

AUTHOR ....

SERIES ....

SERIES BOOK # .... PAGE COUNT ....

GENRE ....

FORMAT ....

START DATE .... FINISH DATE ....

☆☆☆☆☆

PLOT

THOUGHTS

QUOTES

Book Review

TITLE ....

AUTHOR ....

SERIES..

SERIES BOOK #............... PAGE COUNT...............

GENRE..

FORMAT..

START DATE............... FINISH DATE ....

☆☆☆☆☆

PLOT

THOUGHTS

QUOTES

Book Review

TITLE ....

AUTHOR ....

SERIES ....

SERIES BOOK # .... PAGE COUNT ....

GENRE ....

FORMAT ....

START DATE .... FINISH DATE ....

☆☆☆☆☆

PLOT

THOUGHTS

QUOTES

Book Review

TITLE ....

AUTHOR ....

SERIES...

SERIES BOOK #............ PAGE COUNT................

GENRE...

FORMAT...

START DATE................ FINISH DATE ....

☆☆☆☆☆

PLOT

THOUGHTS

QUOTES

Book Review

TITLE ....

AUTHOR ....

SERIES ....

SERIES BOOK # .... PAGE COUNT ....

GENRE ....

FORMAT ....

START DATE .... FINISH DATE ....

☆☆☆☆☆

PLOT

THOUGHTS

QUOTES

Book Review

TITLE ....

AUTHOR ....

SERIES..

SERIES BOOK #............... PAGE COUNT.................

GENRE...

FORMAT..

START DATE................. FINISH DATE ....

☆☆☆☆☆

PLOT

THOUGHTS

QUOTES

Book Review

TITLE ....

AUTHOR ....

SERIES..

SERIES BOOK #............. PAGE COUNT...............

GENRE..

FORMAT..

START DATE.................. FINISH DATE ....

☆☆☆☆☆

PLOT

THOUGHTS

QUOTES

Book Review

TITLE ....

AUTHOR ....

SERIES..

SERIES BOOK #................ PAGE COUNT................

GENRE...

FORMAT...

START DATE................ FINISH DATE ....

☆☆☆☆☆

PLOT

THOUGHTS

QUOTES

Book Review

TITLE ....

AUTHOR ....

SERIES ....

SERIES BOOK # .... PAGE COUNT ....

GENRE ....

FORMAT ....

START DATE .... FINISH DATE ....

☆☆☆☆☆

PLOT

THOUGHTS

QUOTES

Book Review

TITLE ....

AUTHOR ....

SERIES...

SERIES BOOK #.............. PAGE COUNT..............

GENRE..

FORMAT...

START DATE.............. FINISH DATE ....

☆☆☆☆☆

PLOT

THOUGHTS

QUOTES

Book Review

TITLE ....

AUTHOR ....

SERIES ....

SERIES BOOK # .... PAGE COUNT ....

GENRE ....

FORMAT ....

START DATE .... FINISH DATE ....

☆☆☆☆☆

PLOT

THOUGHTS

QUOTES

Book Review

TITLE ....

AUTHOR ....

SERIES...

SERIES BOOK #.............. PAGE COUNT..................

GENRE..

FORMAT..

START DATE............... FINISH DATE ....

☆☆☆☆☆

PLOT

THOUGHTS

QUOTES

Book Review

TITLE ....

AUTHOR ....

SERIES..

SERIES BOOK #............. PAGE COUNT.............

GENRE...

FORMAT..

START DATE.................. FINISH DATE ....

☆☆☆☆☆

PLOT

_____

THOUGHTS

_____

QUOTES

Book Review

TITLE ....

AUTHOR ....

SERIES..

SERIES BOOK #............ PAGE COUNT................

GENRE...

FORMAT...

START DATE................ FINISH DATE ....

☆☆☆☆☆

PLOT

_____

THOUGHTS

_____

QUOTES

Book Review

TITLE ....

AUTHOR ....

SERIES ....

SERIES BOOK # .... PAGE COUNT ....

GENRE ....

FORMAT ....

START DATE .... FINISH DATE ....

☆☆☆☆☆

PLOT

THOUGHTS

QUOTES

Book Review

TITLE ....

AUTHOR ....

SERIES..

SERIES BOOK # .... PAGE COUNT...............

GENRE..

FORMAT..

START DATE................. FINISH DATE ....

☆☆☆☆☆

PLOT

_____

THOUGHTS

_____

QUOTES

Book Review

TITLE ....

AUTHOR ....

SERIES ....

SERIES BOOK # .... PAGE COUNT ....

GENRE ....

FORMAT ....

START DATE .... FINISH DATE ....

☆☆☆☆☆

PLOT

THOUGHTS

QUOTES

Book Review

TITLE ....

AUTHOR ....

SERIES...

SERIES BOOK #............... PAGE COUNT..................

GENRE...

FORMAT...

START DATE.................. FINISH DATE ....

☆☆☆☆☆

PLOT

THOUGHTS

QUOTES

Book Review

TITLE ....

AUTHOR ....

SERIES...

SERIES BOOK #............. PAGE COUNT.............

GENRE...

FORMAT...

START DATE.............. FINISH DATE ....

☆ ☆ ☆ ☆ ☆

PLOT

THOUGHTS

QUOTES

Book Review

TITLE ....

AUTHOR ....

SERIES..

SERIES BOOK #............. PAGE COUNT...............

GENRE..

FORMAT...

START DATE................. FINISH DATE ....

☆☆☆☆☆

PLOT

THOUGHTS

QUOTES

Book Review

TITLE ....

AUTHOR ....

SERIES ....

SERIES BOOK # .... PAGE COUNT ....

GENRE ....

FORMAT ....

START DATE .... FINISH DATE ....

☆☆☆☆☆

PLOT

THOUGHTS

QUOTES

Book Review

TITLE ....

AUTHOR ....

SERIES...

SERIES BOOK #............. PAGE COUNT..................

GENRE...

FORMAT..

START DATE................. FINISH DATE ....

☆☆☆☆☆

PLOT

THOUGHTS

QUOTES

Book Review

TITLE ....

AUTHOR ....

SERIES...

SERIES BOOK #............. PAGE COUNT...............

GENRE...

FORMAT..

START DATE.................. FINISH DATE ....

☆☆☆☆☆

PLOT

THOUGHTS

QUOTES

Book Review

TITLE ....

AUTHOR ....

SERIES ....

SERIES BOOK # .... PAGE COUNT ....

GENRE ....

FORMAT ....

START DATE .... FINISH DATE ....

☆ ☆ ☆ ☆ ☆

PLOT

THOUGHTS

QUOTES

Book Review

TITLE ....

AUTHOR ....

SERIES..

SERIES BOOK #.............. PAGE COUNT...............

GENRE...

FORMAT...

START DATE.................. FINISH DATE ....

PLOT

THOUGHTS

QUOTES

Book Review

TITLE ....

AUTHOR ....

SERIES..

SERIES BOOK #............... PAGE COUNT...............

GENRE..

FORMAT..

START DATE................ FINISH DATE ....

☆ ☆ ☆ ☆ ☆

PLOT

THOUGHTS

QUOTES

Book Review

TITLE ....

AUTHOR ....

SERIES ....

SERIES BOOK # .... PAGE COUNT ....

GENRE ....

FORMAT ....

START DATE .... FINISH DATE ....

☆☆☆☆☆

PLOT

THOUGHTS

QUOTES

Book Review

TITLE ....

AUTHOR ....

SERIES..

SERIES BOOK #............ PAGE COUNT..............

GENRE..

FORMAT...

START DATE................ FINISH DATE ....

☆☆☆☆☆

PLOT

THOUGHTS

QUOTES

Book Review

TITLE ....

AUTHOR ....

SERIES ....

SERIES BOOK # .... PAGE COUNT ....

GENRE ....

FORMAT ....

START DATE .... FINISH DATE ....

☆☆☆☆☆

PLOT

THOUGHTS

QUOTES

Book Review

TITLE ....

AUTHOR ....

SERIES...

SERIES BOOK #............. PAGE COUNT.....................

GENRE..

FORMAT..

START DATE................ FINISH DATE ....

☆☆☆☆☆

PLOT

THOUGHTS

QUOTES

Book Review

TITLE ....

AUTHOR ....

SERIES...

SERIES BOOK # .... PAGE COUNT...............

GENRE ....

FORMAT...

START DATE................. FINISH DATE ....

☆☆☆☆☆

PLOT

THOUGHTS

QUOTES

Book Review

TITLE ....

AUTHOR ....

SERIES...

SERIES BOOK #............ PAGE COUNT.............

GENRE...

FORMAT...

START DATE................ FINISH DATE ....

☆☆☆☆☆

PLOT

THOUGHTS

QUOTES

Book Review

TITLE ....

AUTHOR ....

SERIES..

SERIES BOOK #............ PAGE COUNT.............

GENRE...

FORMAT..

START DATE................ FINISH DATE ....

☆☆☆☆☆

PLOT

THOUGHTS

QUOTES

Book Review

TITLE ....

AUTHOR ....

SERIES...

SERIES BOOK #.............. PAGE COUNT................

GENRE...

FORMAT...

START DATE.................. FINISH DATE ....

☆☆☆☆☆

PLOT

THOUGHTS

QUOTES

Book Review

TITLE ....

AUTHOR ....

SERIES...

SERIES BOOK #.............. PAGE COUNT...............

GENRE..

FORMAT...

START DATE................. FINISH DATE ....

☆ ☆ ☆ ☆ ☆

PLOT

THOUGHTS

QUOTES

Book Review

TITLE ....

AUTHOR ....

SERIES..

SERIES BOOK #............ PAGE COUNT...............

GENRE..

FORMAT..

START DATE................ FINISH DATE ....

☆☆☆☆☆

PLOT

THOUGHTS

QUOTES

Book Review

TITLE ....

AUTHOR ....

SERIES...

SERIES BOOK #.............. PAGE COUNT..............

GENRE..

FORMAT...

START DATE................ FINISH DATE ....

☆☆☆☆☆

PLOT

THOUGHTS

QUOTES

Book Review

TITLE ....

AUTHOR ....

SERIES...

SERIES BOOK #.............. PAGE COUNT.................

GENRE..

FORMAT...

START DATE................. FINISH DATE ....

☆☆☆☆☆

PLOT

THOUGHTS

QUOTES

Book Review

TITLE ....

AUTHOR ....

SERIES ....

SERIES BOOK # .... PAGE COUNT ....

GENRE ....

FORMAT ....

START DATE .... FINISH DATE ....

☆☆☆☆☆

PLOT

THOUGHTS

QUOTES

Book Review

TITLE ....

AUTHOR ....

SERIES..

SERIES BOOK #................ PAGE COUNT...............

GENRE..

FORMAT...

START DATE................ FINISH DATE ....

☆☆☆☆☆

PLOT

THOUGHTS

QUOTES

Book Review

TITLE ....

AUTHOR ....

SERIES ....

SERIES BOOK # .... PAGE COUNT ....

GENRE ....

FORMAT ....

START DATE .... FINISH DATE ....

☆☆☆☆☆

PLOT

THOUGHTS

QUOTES

Book Review

TITLE ....

AUTHOR ....

SERIES..

SERIES BOOK #................. PAGE COUNT................

GENRE...

FORMAT...

START DATE.................. FINISH DATE ....

PLOT

THOUGHTS

QUOTES

Book Review

TITLE ....

AUTHOR ....

SERIES...

SERIES BOOK #............... PAGE COUNT...............

GENRE..

FORMAT...

START DATE................. FINISH DATE ....

☆☆☆☆☆

PLOT

THOUGHTS

QUOTES

Book Review

TITLE ....

AUTHOR ....

SERIES..

SERIES BOOK #............. PAGE COUNT...............

GENRE...

FORMAT...

START DATE................. FINISH DATE ....

☆☆☆☆☆

PLOT

THOUGHTS

QUOTES

Book Review

TITLE ....

AUTHOR ....

SERIES...

SERIES BOOK #............. PAGE COUNT...............

GENRE..

FORMAT..

START DATE.................. FINISH DATE ....

☆☆☆☆☆

PLOT

THOUGHTS

QUOTES

Book Review

TITLE ....

AUTHOR ....

SERIES..

SERIES BOOK #............. PAGE COUNT.............

GENRE ....

FORMAT..

START DATE................ FINISH DATE ....

☆☆☆☆☆

PLOT

THOUGHTS

QUOTES

Book Review

TITLE ....

AUTHOR ....

SERIES..

SERIES BOOK #............. PAGE COUNT.............

GENRE..

FORMAT..

START DATE.............. FINISH DATE ....

☆☆☆☆☆

PLOT

THOUGHTS

QUOTES

Book Review

TITLE ....

AUTHOR ....

SERIES...

SERIES BOOK #.............. PAGE COUNT..............

GENRE...

FORMAT...

START DATE................. FINISH DATE ....

☆☆☆☆☆

PLOT

_____

THOUGHTS

_____

QUOTES

Book Review

TITLE ....

AUTHOR ....

SERIES...

SERIES BOOK #.............. PAGE COUNT................

GENRE...

FORMAT..

START DATE.................. FINISH DATE ....

☆☆☆☆☆

PLOT

_____

THOUGHTS

_____

QUOTES

Book Review

TITLE ....

AUTHOR ....

SERIES...

SERIES BOOK #.............. PAGE COUNT.................

GENRE..

FORMAT..

START DATE.................. FINISH DATE ....

☆☆☆☆☆

PLOT

THOUGHTS

QUOTES

Book Review

TITLE ....

AUTHOR ....

SERIES...

SERIES BOOK #................ PAGE COUNT................

GENRE..

FORMAT...

START DATE.................. FINISH DATE ....

☆☆☆☆☆

PLOT

THOUGHTS

QUOTES

Book Review

TITLE ....

AUTHOR ....

SERIES...

SERIES BOOK #............... PAGE COUNT...............

GENRE...

FORMAT..

START DATE................. FINISH DATE ....

☆☆☆☆☆

PLOT

THOUGHTS

QUOTES

Book Review

TITLE ....

AUTHOR ....

SERIES ....

SERIES BOOK # .... PAGE COUNT ....

GENRE ....

FORMAT ....

START DATE .... FINISH DATE ....

☆☆☆☆☆

PLOT

THOUGHTS

QUOTES

Book Review

TITLE ....

AUTHOR ....

SERIES..

SERIES BOOK #.............. PAGE COUNT................

GENRE..

FORMAT..

START DATE................. FINISH DATE ....

☆☆☆☆☆

PLOT

THOUGHTS

QUOTES

Book Review

TITLE ....

AUTHOR ....

SERIES..

SERIES BOOK #.............. PAGE COUNT...............

GENRE..

FORMAT...

START DATE............... FINISH DATE ....

☆☆☆☆☆

PLOT

THOUGHTS

QUOTES

Book Review

TITLE ....

AUTHOR ....

SERIES...

SERIES BOOK #.............. PAGE COUNT..............

GENRE..

FORMAT...

START DATE.............. FINISH DATE ....

☆☆☆☆☆

PLOT

THOUGHTS

QUOTES

Book Review

TITLE ....
AUTHOR ....
SERIES ....
SERIES BOOK # .... PAGE COUNT ....
GENRE ....
FORMAT ....
START DATE .... FINISH DATE ....

☆☆☆☆☆

PLOT

THOUGHTS

QUOTES

Book Review

TITLE ....

AUTHOR ....

SERIES..

SERIES BOOK #.............. PAGE COUNT...............

GENRE...

FORMAT...

START DATE................. FINISH DATE ....

☆☆☆☆☆

PLOT

THOUGHTS

QUOTES

Book Review

TITLE ....

AUTHOR ....

SERIES ....

SERIES BOOK # .... PAGE COUNT ....

GENRE ....

FORMAT ....

START DATE .... FINISH DATE ....

☆☆☆☆☆

PLOT

THOUGHTS

QUOTES

Book Review

TITLE ....

AUTHOR ....

SERIES...

SERIES BOOK #............. PAGE COUNT...............

GENRE...

FORMAT...

START DATE................. FINISH DATE ....

☆☆☆☆☆

PLOT

_____

THOUGHTS

_____

QUOTES

Book Review

TITLE ....

AUTHOR ....

SERIES..

SERIES BOOK #.............. PAGE COUNT..............

GENRE..

FORMAT...

START DATE.............. FINISH DATE ....

☆☆☆☆☆

PLOT

THOUGHTS

QUOTES

Book Review

TITLE ....

AUTHOR ....

SERIES..

SERIES BOOK #............. PAGE COUNT...............

GENRE..

FORMAT...

START DATE................. FINISH DATE ....

☆☆☆☆☆

PLOT

THOUGHTS

QUOTES

Book Review

TITLE ....

AUTHOR ....

SERIES..

SERIES BOOK #............. PAGE COUNT.............

GENRE...

FORMAT..

START DATE................ FINISH DATE ....

☆☆☆☆☆

PLOT

THOUGHTS

QUOTES

Book Review

TITLE ....

AUTHOR ....

SERIES..

SERIES BOOK #................. PAGE COUNT.................

GENRE..

FORMAT...

START DATE.................. FINISH DATE ....

☆☆☆☆☆

PLOT

THOUGHTS

QUOTES

Book Review

TITLE ....

AUTHOR ....

SERIES...

SERIES BOOK #.............. PAGE COUNT...............

GENRE...

FORMAT...

START DATE................. FINISH DATE ....

☆☆☆☆☆

PLOT

THOUGHTS

QUOTES

Book Review

TITLE ....

AUTHOR ....

SERIES...

SERIES BOOK #............ PAGE COUNT...............

GENRE..

FORMAT..

START DATE................. FINISH DATE ....

☆☆☆☆☆

PLOT

THOUGHTS

QUOTES

Book Review

TITLE ....

AUTHOR ....

SERIES ....

SERIES BOOK # .... PAGE COUNT ....

GENRE ....

FORMAT ....

START DATE .... FINISH DATE ....

☆☆☆☆☆

PLOT

THOUGHTS

QUOTES

Book Review

TITLE ....

AUTHOR ....

SERIES..

SERIES BOOK #............... PAGE COUNT................

GENRE...

FORMAT..

START DATE.................. FINISH DATE ....

☆☆☆☆☆

PLOT

THOUGHTS

QUOTES

Book Review

TITLE ....

AUTHOR ....

SERIES ....

SERIES BOOK # .... PAGE COUNT ....

GENRE ....

FORMAT ....

START DATE .... FINISH DATE ....

☆☆☆☆☆

PLOT

THOUGHTS

QUOTES

Book Review

TITLE ....

AUTHOR ....

SERIES ....

SERIES BOOK # .... PAGE COUNT ....

GENRE ....

FORMAT ....

START DATE .... FINISH DATE ....

☆☆☆☆☆

PLOT

THOUGHTS

QUOTES

Book Review

TITLE ....

AUTHOR ....

SERIES ....

SERIES BOOK # .... PAGE COUNT ....

GENRE ....

FORMAT ....

START DATE .... FINISH DATE ....

☆☆☆☆☆

PLOT
_____

THOUGHTS
_____

QUOTES

Book Review

TITLE ....

AUTHOR ....

SERIES..

SERIES BOOK #............. PAGE COUNT................

GENRE..

FORMAT..

START DATE................. FINISH DATE ....

☆☆☆☆☆

PLOT

_____

THOUGHTS

_____

QUOTES

Book Review

TITLE ....

AUTHOR ....

SERIES...

SERIES BOOK #............. PAGE COUNT...............

GENRE...

FORMAT...

START DATE............... FINISH DATE ....

☆☆☆☆☆

PLOT

THOUGHTS

QUOTES

Book Review

TITLE ....

AUTHOR ....

SERIES..

SERIES BOOK #............ PAGE COUNT..............

GENRE...

FORMAT...

START DATE................ FINISH DATE ....

☆☆☆☆☆

PLOT

_____

THOUGHTS

_____

QUOTES

Book Review

TITLE ....

AUTHOR ....

SERIES..

SERIES BOOK #............. PAGE COUNT.............

GENRE...

FORMAT...

START DATE................. FINISH DATE ....

☆☆☆☆☆

PLOT

THOUGHTS

QUOTES

Book Review

TITLE ....

AUTHOR ....

SERIES...

SERIES BOOK #............. PAGE COUNT................

GENRE...

FORMAT..

START DATE................. FINISH DATE ....

☆☆☆☆☆

PLOT

THOUGHTS

QUOTES

Book Review

TITLE ....

AUTHOR ....

SERIES...

SERIES BOOK #............... PAGE COUNT...............

GENRE..

FORMAT...

START DATE................ FINISH DATE ....

☆☆☆☆☆

PLOT

THOUGHTS

QUOTES

Book Review

TITLE ....

AUTHOR ....

SERIES..

SERIES BOOK #............. PAGE COUNT...............

GENRE...

FORMAT..

START DATE................. FINISH DATE ....

PLOT

THOUGHTS

QUOTES

Book Review

TITLE ....

AUTHOR ....

SERIES..

SERIES BOOK #............... PAGE COUNT...............

GENRE..

FORMAT..

START DATE................. FINISH DATE ....

☆☆☆☆☆

PLOT

THOUGHTS

QUOTES

Book Review

TITLE ....

AUTHOR ....

SERIES...

SERIES BOOK #.............. PAGE COUNT...............

GENRE...

FORMAT..

START DATE................ FINISH DATE ....

☆☆☆☆☆

PLOT

THOUGHTS

QUOTES

Book Review

TITLE ....

AUTHOR ....

SERIES ....

SERIES BOOK # .... PAGE COUNT ....

GENRE ....

FORMAT ....

START DATE .... FINISH DATE ....

☆☆☆☆☆

PLOT

_____

THOUGHTS

_____

QUOTES

Book Review

TITLE ....

AUTHOR ....

SERIES..

SERIES BOOK #................... PAGE COUNT...................

GENRE..

FORMAT...

START DATE................... FINISH DATE ....

☆☆☆☆☆

PLOT

THOUGHTS

QUOTES

Book Review

TITLE ....

AUTHOR ....

SERIES ....

SERIES BOOK # .... PAGE COUNT ....

GENRE ....

FORMAT ....

START DATE .... FINISH DATE ....

☆☆☆☆☆

PLOT

_____

THOUGHTS

_____

QUOTES

Book Review

TITLE ....

AUTHOR ....

SERIES..

SERIES BOOK #............... PAGE COUNT...............

GENRE...

FORMAT...

START DATE................. FINISH DATE ....

☆☆☆☆☆

PLOT

THOUGHTS

QUOTES

Book Review

TITLE ....

AUTHOR ....

SERIES ....

SERIES BOOK # .... PAGE COUNT ....

GENRE ....

FORMAT ....

START DATE .... FINISH DATE ....

☆☆☆☆☆

PLOT

THOUGHTS

QUOTES

Book Review

TITLE ....

AUTHOR ....

SERIES..

SERIES BOOK #............... PAGE COUNT...............

GENRE..

FORMAT..

START DATE................. FINISH DATE ....

☆☆☆☆☆

PLOT

THOUGHTS

QUOTES

Book Review

TITLE ....

AUTHOR ....

SERIES...

SERIES BOOK #............... PAGE COUNT...............

GENRE..

FORMAT...

START DATE................ FINISH DATE ....

PLOT

THOUGHTS

QUOTES

Book Review

TITLE ....

AUTHOR ....

SERIES ....

SERIES BOOK # .... PAGE COUNT ....

GENRE ....

FORMAT ....

START DATE .... FINISH DATE ....

☆☆☆☆☆

PLOT

THOUGHTS

QUOTES

Book Review

TITLE ....

AUTHOR ....

SERIES...

SERIES BOOK #............... PAGE COUNT...............

GENRE...

FORMAT...

START DATE................. FINISH DATE ....

☆☆☆☆☆

PLOT

THOUGHTS

QUOTES

Book Review

TITLE ....

AUTHOR ....

SERIES..

SERIES BOOK #............. PAGE COUNT................

GENRE..

FORMAT..

START DATE................. FINISH DATE ....

☆☆☆☆☆

PLOT

_____

THOUGHTS

_____

QUOTES

Book Review

TITLE ....

AUTHOR ....

SERIES ....

SERIES BOOK # .... PAGE COUNT ....

GENRE ....

FORMAT ....

START DATE .... FINISH DATE ....

☆ ☆ ☆ ☆ ☆

PLOT

THOUGHTS

QUOTES

Book Review

TITLE ....

AUTHOR ....

SERIES...

SERIES BOOK #............. PAGE COUNT.................

GENRE..

FORMAT..

START DATE.................. FINISH DATE ....

☆☆☆☆☆

PLOT

THOUGHTS

QUOTES

Book Review

TITLE ....

AUTHOR ....

SERIES...

SERIES BOOK #................ PAGE COUNT................

GENRE..

FORMAT...

START DATE................. FINISH DATE ....

☆☆☆☆☆

PLOT

_____

THOUGHTS

_____

QUOTES

Book Review

TITLE ....

AUTHOR ....

SERIES...

SERIES BOOK #............. PAGE COUNT...............

GENRE...

FORMAT...

START DATE................ FINISH DATE ....

☆☆☆☆☆

PLOT

_____

THOUGHTS

_____

QUOTES

Book Review

TITLE ....

AUTHOR ....

SERIES..

SERIES BOOK #............... PAGE COUNT...............

GENRE...

FORMAT...

START DATE................. FINISH DATE ....

☆☆☆☆☆

PLOT

THOUGHTS

QUOTES

Book Review

TITLE ....

AUTHOR ....

SERIES...

SERIES BOOK #............... PAGE COUNT...............

GENRE...

FORMAT...

START DATE................. FINISH DATE ....

PLOT

THOUGHTS

QUOTES

Book Review

TITLE ....

AUTHOR ....

SERIES ....

SERIES BOOK # .... PAGE COUNT ....

GENRE ....

FORMAT ....

START DATE .... FINISH DATE ....

☆☆☆☆☆

PLOT

THOUGHTS

QUOTES

Book Review

TITLE ....

AUTHOR ....

SERIES..

SERIES BOOK #.............. PAGE COUNT..............

GENRE..

FORMAT...

START DATE................. FINISH DATE ....

☆☆☆☆☆

PLOT

THOUGHTS

QUOTES

Book Review

TITLE ....

AUTHOR ....

SERIES ....

SERIES BOOK # .... PAGE COUNT ....

GENRE ....

FORMAT ....

START DATE .... FINISH DATE ....

☆☆☆☆☆

PLOT

THOUGHTS

QUOTES

Book Review

TITLE ....

AUTHOR ....

SERIES ....

SERIES BOOK # .... PAGE COUNT ....

GENRE ....

FORMAT ....

START DATE .... FINISH DATE ....

☆☆☆☆☆

PLOT

THOUGHTS

QUOTES

Book Review

TITLE ....

AUTHOR ....

SERIES...

SERIES BOOK #............... PAGE COUNT...............

GENRE...

FORMAT...

START DATE.................. FINISH DATE ....

☆☆☆☆☆

PLOT

THOUGHTS

QUOTES

Book Review

TITLE ....

AUTHOR ....

SERIES..

SERIES BOOK #............. PAGE COUNT.............

GENRE...

FORMAT..

START DATE.............. FINISH DATE ....

☆☆☆☆☆

PLOT

THOUGHTS

QUOTES

Book Review

TITLE ....

AUTHOR ....

SERIES ....

SERIES BOOK # .... PAGE COUNT ....

GENRE ....

FORMAT ....

START DATE .... FINISH DATE ....

☆☆☆☆☆

PLOT

_____

THOUGHTS

_____

QUOTES

Book Review

TITLE ....

AUTHOR ....

SERIES..

SERIES BOOK #................ PAGE COUNT................

GENRE..

FORMAT...

START DATE.................. FINISH DATE ....

☆☆☆☆☆

PLOT

THOUGHTS

QUOTES

Book Review

TITLE ....
AUTHOR ....
SERIES ....
SERIES BOOK # .... PAGE COUNT ....
GENRE ....
FORMAT ....
START DATE .... FINISH DATE ....

☆☆☆☆☆

PLOT

THOUGHTS

QUOTES

Book Review

TITLE ....

AUTHOR ....

SERIES...

SERIES BOOK #............... PAGE COUNT...............

GENRE..

FORMAT..

START DATE.................. FINISH DATE ....

☆☆☆☆☆

PLOT

THOUGHTS

QUOTES

Book Review

TITLE ....

AUTHOR ....

SERIES...

SERIES BOOK #............. PAGE COUNT...............

GENRE...

FORMAT..

START DATE................. FINISH DATE ....

☆☆☆☆☆

PLOT

_____

THOUGHTS

_____

QUOTES

Book Review

TITLE ....

AUTHOR ....

SERIES...

SERIES BOOK #............... PAGE COUNT...............

GENRE..

FORMAT...

START DATE................. FINISH DATE ....

☆☆☆☆☆

PLOT

THOUGHTS

QUOTES

Book Review

TITLE ....

AUTHOR ....

SERIES..

SERIES BOOK #.............. PAGE COUNT...............

GENRE..

FORMAT...

START DATE................ FINISH DATE ....

☆☆☆☆☆

PLOT

THOUGHTS

QUOTES

Book Review

TITLE ....

AUTHOR ....

SERIES...

SERIES BOOK #............. PAGE COUNT...............

GENRE...

FORMAT..

START DATE................. FINISH DATE ....

☆☆☆☆☆

PLOT

_____

THOUGHTS

_____

QUOTES

Book Review

TITLE ....

AUTHOR ....

SERIES ....

SERIES BOOK # .... PAGE COUNT ....

GENRE ....

FORMAT ....

START DATE .... FINISH DATE ....

☆☆☆☆☆

PLOT

THOUGHTS

QUOTES

Book Review

TITLE ....

AUTHOR ....

SERIES...

SERIES BOOK #............... PAGE COUNT...............

GENRE...

FORMAT...

START DATE................. FINISH DATE ....

☆☆☆☆☆

PLOT

THOUGHTS

QUOTES

Book Review

TITLE ....

AUTHOR ....

SERIES ....

SERIES BOOK # .... PAGE COUNT ....

GENRE ....

FORMAT ....

START DATE .... FINISH DATE ....

☆☆☆☆☆

PLOT

THOUGHTS

QUOTES

Book Review

TITLE ....

AUTHOR ....

SERIES...

SERIES BOOK #.............. PAGE COUNT...............

GENRE...

FORMAT...

START DATE................. FINISH DATE ....

☆☆☆☆☆

PLOT

THOUGHTS

QUOTES

Book Review

TITLE ....

AUTHOR ....

SERIES...

SERIES BOOK #.............. PAGE COUNT...............

GENRE...

FORMAT..

START DATE................. FINISH DATE ....

PLOT

THOUGHTS

QUOTES

Book Review

TITLE ....

AUTHOR ....

SERIES..

SERIES BOOK #................ PAGE COUNT................

GENRE...

FORMAT...

START DATE.................. FINISH DATE ....

☆☆☆☆☆

PLOT

THOUGHTS

QUOTES

Book Review

TITLE ....

AUTHOR ....

SERIES...

SERIES BOOK #............. PAGE COUNT...............

GENRE...

FORMAT...

START DATE................. FINISH DATE ....

☆☆☆☆☆

PLOT

THOUGHTS

QUOTES

Book Review

TITLE ....

AUTHOR ....

SERIES ....

SERIES BOOK # .... PAGE COUNT ....

GENRE ....

FORMAT ....

START DATE .... FINISH DATE ....

☆☆☆☆☆

PLOT

THOUGHTS

QUOTES

Book Review

TITLE ....

AUTHOR ....

SERIES ....

SERIES BOOK # .... PAGE COUNT ....

GENRE ....

FORMAT ....

START DATE .... FINISH DATE ....

☆☆☆☆☆

PLOT

THOUGHTS

QUOTES

Book Review

TITLE ....

AUTHOR ....

SERIES..

SERIES BOOK #.............. PAGE COUNT................

GENRE...

FORMAT..

START DATE.................. FINISH DATE ....

☆☆☆☆☆

PLOT

THOUGHTS

QUOTES

Book Review

TITLE ....

AUTHOR ....

SERIES ....

SERIES BOOK # .... PAGE COUNT ....

GENRE ....

FORMAT ....

START DATE .... FINISH DATE ....

☆☆☆☆☆

PLOT

THOUGHTS

QUOTES

Book Review

TITLE ....

AUTHOR ....

SERIES..

SERIES BOOK #............. PAGE COUNT...............

GENRE..

FORMAT..

START DATE................. FINISH DATE ....

☆☆☆☆☆

PLOT

THOUGHTS

QUOTES

Book Review

TITLE ....

AUTHOR ....

SERIES..

SERIES BOOK #.............. PAGE COUNT...............

GENRE..

FORMAT..

START DATE.............. FINISH DATE ....

☆☆☆☆☆

PLOT

THOUGHTS

QUOTES

Book Review

TITLE ....

AUTHOR ....

SERIES..

SERIES BOOK #.............. PAGE COUNT...............

GENRE...

FORMAT...

START DATE................. FINISH DATE ....

☆☆☆☆☆

PLOT

THOUGHTS

QUOTES

Book Review

TITLE ....

AUTHOR ....

SERIES..

SERIES BOOK #............... PAGE COUNT...............

GENRE...

FORMAT...

START DATE.................. FINISH DATE ....

☆☆☆☆☆

PLOT

THOUGHTS

QUOTES

Book Review

TITLE ....

AUTHOR ....

SERIES..

SERIES BOOK #.............. PAGE COUNT..............

GENRE..

FORMAT...

START DATE................ FINISH DATE ....

☆☆☆☆☆

PLOT

THOUGHTS

QUOTES

Book Review

TITLE ....

AUTHOR ....

SERIES..

SERIES BOOK #............. PAGE COUNT..............

GENRE..

FORMAT...

START DATE................. FINISH DATE ....

☆☆☆☆☆

PLOT

THOUGHTS

QUOTES

Book Review

TITLE ....

AUTHOR ....

SERIES..

SERIES BOOK #............ PAGE COUNT...............

GENRE..

FORMAT...

START DATE................ FINISH DATE ....

☆☆☆☆☆

PLOT

THOUGHTS

QUOTES

Book Review

TITLE ....

AUTHOR ....

SERIES ....

SERIES BOOK # .... PAGE COUNT ....

GENRE ....

FORMAT ....

START DATE .... FINISH DATE ....

PLOT

THOUGHTS

QUOTES

Book Review

TITLE ....

AUTHOR ....

SERIES...

SERIES BOOK #............. PAGE COUNT.............

GENRE..

FORMAT...

START DATE................. FINISH DATE ....

PLOT

THOUGHTS

QUOTES

Book Review

TITLE ....

AUTHOR ....

SERIES ....

SERIES BOOK # .... PAGE COUNT ....

GENRE ....

FORMAT ....

START DATE .... FINISH DATE ....

☆☆☆☆☆

PLOT

THOUGHTS

QUOTES

Book Review

TITLE ....

AUTHOR ....

SERIES..

SERIES BOOK #............... PAGE COUNT................

GENRE...

FORMAT..

START DATE................. FINISH DATE ....

☆☆☆☆☆

PLOT

THOUGHTS

QUOTES

Book Review

TITLE ....

AUTHOR ....

SERIES ....

SERIES BOOK # .... PAGE COUNT ....

GENRE ....

FORMAT ....

START DATE .... FINISH DATE ....

☆☆☆☆☆

PLOT

THOUGHTS

QUOTES

Book Review

TITLE ....

AUTHOR ....

SERIES...

SERIES BOOK #.............. PAGE COUNT...............

GENRE...

FORMAT..

START DATE................ FINISH DATE ....

☆☆☆☆☆

PLOT

THOUGHTS

QUOTES

Book Review

TITLE ....

AUTHOR ....

SERIES...

SERIES BOOK #.................. PAGE COUNT...............

GENRE..

FORMAT..

START DATE................... FINISH DATE ....

PLOT

THOUGHTS

QUOTES

Book Review

TITLE ....

AUTHOR ....

SERIES...

SERIES BOOK #............. PAGE COUNT...............

GENRE...

FORMAT...

START DATE................. FINISH DATE ....

☆☆☆☆☆

PLOT

THOUGHTS

QUOTES

Book Review

TITLE ....

AUTHOR ....

SERIES...

SERIES BOOK #............... PAGE COUNT...............

GENRE...

FORMAT..

START DATE................. FINISH DATE ....

☆☆☆☆☆

PLOT

THOUGHTS

QUOTES

Book Review

TITLE ....

AUTHOR ....

SERIES ....

SERIES BOOK # .... PAGE COUNT ....

GENRE ....

FORMAT ....

START DATE .... FINISH DATE ....

☆☆☆☆☆

PLOT

THOUGHTS

QUOTES

Book Review

TITLE ....

AUTHOR ....

SERIES...

SERIES BOOK #............... PAGE COUNT................

GENRE...

FORMAT..

START DATE................. FINISH DATE ....

☆☆☆☆☆

PLOT

THOUGHTS

QUOTES

Book Review

TITLE ....

AUTHOR ....

SERIES..

SERIES BOOK #.............. PAGE COUNT...............

GENRE...

FORMAT..

START DATE................. FINISH DATE ....

☆☆☆☆☆

PLOT

_____

THOUGHTS

_____

QUOTES

Book Review

TITLE ....

AUTHOR ....

SERIES ....

SERIES BOOK # .... PAGE COUNT ....

GENRE ....

FORMAT ....

START DATE .... FINISH DATE ....

☆☆☆☆☆

PLOT

THOUGHTS

QUOTES

Book Review

TITLE ....

AUTHOR ....

SERIES..

SERIES BOOK #............. PAGE COUNT...............

GENRE...

FORMAT...

START DATE................. FINISH DATE ....

☆☆☆☆☆

PLOT

_____

THOUGHTS

_____

QUOTES

Book Review

TITLE ....

AUTHOR ....

SERIES...

SERIES BOOK #................ PAGE COUNT...............

GENRE..

FORMAT..

START DATE................. FINISH DATE ....

☆☆☆☆☆

PLOT

THOUGHTS

QUOTES

Book Review

TITLE ....

AUTHOR ....

SERIES...

SERIES BOOK #................ PAGE COUNT................

GENRE...

FORMAT..

START DATE.................. FINISH DATE ....

☆☆☆☆☆

PLOT

THOUGHTS

QUOTES

Book Review

TITLE ....

AUTHOR ....

SERIES ....

SERIES BOOK # .... PAGE COUNT ....

GENRE ....

FORMAT ....

START DATE .... FINISH DATE ....

☆☆☆☆☆

PLOT

THOUGHTS

QUOTES

Book Review

TITLE ....

AUTHOR ....

SERIES...

SERIES BOOK #................ PAGE COUNT.................

GENRE...

FORMAT..

START DATE.................. FINISH DATE ....

☆☆☆☆☆

PLOT

THOUGHTS

QUOTES

Book Review

TITLE ....

AUTHOR ....

SERIES...

SERIES BOOK #............... PAGE COUNT................

GENRE...

FORMAT..

START DATE................. FINISH DATE ....

☆ ☆ ☆ ☆ ☆

PLOT

THOUGHTS

QUOTES

Book Review

TITLE ....

AUTHOR ....

SERIES ....

SERIES BOOK # .... PAGE COUNT ....

GENRE ....

FORMAT ....

START DATE .... FINISH DATE ....

☆☆☆☆☆

PLOT

THOUGHTS

QUOTES

Book Review

TITLE ....

AUTHOR ....

SERIES ....

SERIES BOOK # .... PAGE COUNT ....

GENRE ....

FORMAT ....

START DATE .... FINISH DATE ....

☆☆☆☆☆

PLOT

_____

THOUGHTS

_____

QUOTES

Book Review

TITLE ....

AUTHOR ....

SERIES..

SERIES BOOK #............. PAGE COUNT...............

GENRE...

FORMAT..

START DATE................. FINISH DATE ....

☆☆☆☆☆

PLOT

THOUGHTS

QUOTES

Book Review

TITLE ....

AUTHOR ....

SERIES...

SERIES BOOK #............. PAGE COUNT................

GENRE...

FORMAT..

START DATE................. FINISH DATE ....

☆☆☆☆☆

PLOT

THOUGHTS

QUOTES

Book Review

TITLE ....

AUTHOR ....

SERIES...

SERIES BOOK #............. PAGE COUNT.............

GENRE...

FORMAT..

START DATE................. FINISH DATE ....

☆☆☆☆☆

PLOT

_____

THOUGHTS

_____

QUOTES

Book Review

TITLE ....

AUTHOR ....

SERIES ....

SERIES BOOK # .... PAGE COUNT ....

GENRE ....

FORMAT ....

START DATE .... FINISH DATE ....

☆☆☆☆☆

PLOT

THOUGHTS

QUOTES

Book Review

TITLE ....

AUTHOR ....

SERIES...

SERIES BOOK #................. PAGE COUNT.................

GENRE...

FORMAT...

START DATE.................. FINISH DATE ....

☆☆☆☆☆

PLOT

THOUGHTS

QUOTES

Book Review

TITLE ....
AUTHOR ....
SERIES ....
SERIES BOOK # .... PAGE COUNT ....
GENRE ....
FORMAT ....
START DATE .... FINISH DATE ....

☆☆☆☆☆

PLOT

THOUGHTS

QUOTES

Book Review

TITLE ....

AUTHOR ....

SERIES...

SERIES BOOK #............. PAGE COUNT...............

GENRE..

FORMAT..

START DATE................. FINISH DATE ....

☆☆☆☆☆

PLOT

THOUGHTS

QUOTES

Book Review

TITLE ....

AUTHOR ....

SERIES ....

SERIES BOOK # .... PAGE COUNT ....

GENRE ....

FORMAT ....

START DATE .... FINISH DATE ....

☆☆☆☆☆

PLOT

_____

THOUGHTS

_____

QUOTES

Book Review

TITLE ....

AUTHOR ....

SERIES..

SERIES BOOK #............. PAGE COUNT...............

GENRE...

FORMAT...

START DATE................ FINISH DATE ....

☆☆☆☆☆

PLOT

THOUGHTS

QUOTES

Book Review

TITLE ....

AUTHOR ....

SERIES ....

SERIES BOOK # .... PAGE COUNT ....

GENRE ....

FORMAT ....

START DATE .... FINISH DATE ....

☆☆☆☆☆

PLOT

THOUGHTS

QUOTES

Book Review

TITLE ....

AUTHOR ....

SERIES...

SERIES BOOK #............. PAGE COUNT...............

GENRE...

FORMAT...

START DATE................. FINISH DATE ....

☆☆☆☆☆

PLOT

THOUGHTS

QUOTES

Book Review

TITLE ....

AUTHOR ....

SERIES...

SERIES BOOK #.............. PAGE COUNT................

GENRE..

FORMAT...

START DATE................. FINISH DATE ....

☆☆☆☆☆

PLOT

THOUGHTS

QUOTES

Book Review

TITLE ....

AUTHOR ....

SERIES..

SERIES BOOK #................. PAGE COUNT..................

GENRE...

FORMAT..

START DATE................. FINISH DATE ....

☆☆☆☆☆

PLOT

THOUGHTS

QUOTES

Book Review

TITLE ....

AUTHOR ....

SERIES...

SERIES BOOK #............. PAGE COUNT..............

GENRE...

FORMAT...

START DATE................ FINISH DATE ....

☆☆☆☆☆

PLOT

THOUGHTS

QUOTES

Book Review

TITLE ....
AUTHOR ....
SERIES...
SERIES BOOK #............ PAGE COUNT...............
GENRE...
FORMAT...
START DATE................. FINISH DATE ....

☆☆☆☆☆

PLOT

THOUGHTS

QUOTES

Book Review

TITLE ....

AUTHOR ....

SERIES ....

SERIES BOOK # .... PAGE COUNT ....

GENRE ....

FORMAT ....

START DATE .... FINISH DATE ....

☆☆☆☆☆

PLOT

_____

THOUGHTS

_____

QUOTES

Book Review

TITLE ....

AUTHOR ....

SERIES ....

SERIES BOOK # .... PAGE COUNT ....

GENRE ....

FORMAT ....

START DATE .... FINISH DATE ....

☆☆☆☆☆

PLOT

THOUGHTS

QUOTES

Book Review

TITLE ....

AUTHOR ....

SERIES ....

SERIES BOOK # .... PAGE COUNT ....

GENRE ....

FORMAT ....

START DATE .... FINISH DATE ....

☆☆☆☆☆

PLOT

THOUGHTS

QUOTES

Book Review

TITLE ....

AUTHOR ....

SERIES..

SERIES BOOK #............. PAGE COUNT...............

GENRE..

FORMAT..

START DATE................. FINISH DATE ....

☆☆☆☆☆

PLOT

THOUGHTS

QUOTES

Book Review

TITLE ....

AUTHOR ....

SERIES..

SERIES BOOK #............. PAGE COUNT..............

GENRE...

FORMAT..

START DATE................. FINISH DATE ....

☆☆☆☆☆

PLOT

THOUGHTS

QUOTES

Book Review

TITLE ....

AUTHOR ....

SERIES...

SERIES BOOK #............. PAGE COUNT..............

GENRE..

FORMAT...

START DATE................. FINISH DATE ....

☆☆☆☆☆

PLOT

_____

THOUGHTS

_____

QUOTES

Book Review

TITLE ....

AUTHOR ....

SERIES...

SERIES BOOK #............... PAGE COUNT...............

GENRE..

FORMAT...

START DATE................ FINISH DATE ....

☆☆☆☆☆

PLOT

THOUGHTS

QUOTES

Book Review

TITLE ....

AUTHOR ....

SERIES...

SERIES BOOK #.............. PAGE COUNT...............

GENRE...

FORMAT..

START DATE................ FINISH DATE ....

☆☆☆☆☆

PLOT

THOUGHTS

QUOTES

Book Review

TITLE ....

AUTHOR ....

SERIES ....

SERIES BOOK # .... PAGE COUNT ....

GENRE ....

FORMAT ....

START DATE .... FINISH DATE ....

☆☆☆☆☆

PLOT

THOUGHTS

QUOTES

Book Review

TITLE ....

AUTHOR ....

SERIES ....

SERIES BOOK # .... PAGE COUNT ....

GENRE ....

FORMAT ....

START DATE .... FINISH DATE ....

☆☆☆☆☆

PLOT

_____

THOUGHTS

_____

QUOTES

Book Review

TITLE ....

AUTHOR ....

SERIES..

SERIES BOOK #............... PAGE COUNT...............

GENRE...

FORMAT..

START DATE................. FINISH DATE ....

☆☆☆☆☆

PLOT

THOUGHTS

QUOTES

Book Review

TITLE ....

AUTHOR ....

SERIES..

SERIES BOOK #............. PAGE COUNT...............

GENRE...

FORMAT...

START DATE................. FINISH DATE ....

☆☆☆☆☆

PLOT

THOUGHTS

QUOTES

Book Review

TITLE ....

AUTHOR ....

SERIES ....

SERIES BOOK # .... PAGE COUNT ....

GENRE ....

FORMAT ....

START DATE .... FINISH DATE ....

☆☆☆☆☆

PLOT

THOUGHTS

QUOTES

Book Review

TITLE ....

AUTHOR ....

SERIES..

SERIES BOOK #............... PAGE COUNT...............

GENRE...

FORMAT..

START DATE................. FINISH DATE ....

☆☆☆☆☆

PLOT

_____

THOUGHTS

_____

QUOTES

Book Review

TITLE ....

AUTHOR ....

SERIES...

SERIES BOOK #................ PAGE COUNT................

GENRE..

FORMAT...

START DATE.................. FINISH DATE ....

☆☆☆☆☆

PLOT

THOUGHTS

QUOTES

Book Review

TITLE ....

AUTHOR ....

SERIES..

SERIES BOOK #............. PAGE COUNT...............

GENRE..

FORMAT..

START DATE................. FINISH DATE ....

☆☆☆☆☆

PLOT

THOUGHTS

QUOTES

Book Review

TITLE ....

AUTHOR ....

SERIES..

SERIES BOOK #............... PAGE COUNT...............

GENRE..

FORMAT..

START DATE................. FINISH DATE ....

⭐⭐⭐⭐⭐

PLOT

THOUGHTS

QUOTES

Book Review

TITLE ....

AUTHOR ....

SERIES...

SERIES BOOK #............. PAGE COUNT...............

GENRE...

FORMAT..

START DATE................ FINISH DATE ....

☆☆☆☆☆

PLOT

THOUGHTS

QUOTES

Book Review

TITLE ....

AUTHOR ....

SERIES...

SERIES BOOK #............... PAGE COUNT...............

GENRE..

FORMAT...

START DATE.................. FINISH DATE ....

☆☆☆☆☆

PLOT

THOUGHTS

QUOTES

Book Review

TITLE ....

AUTHOR ....

SERIES...

SERIES BOOK #............. PAGE COUNT...............

GENRE..

FORMAT...

START DATE................. FINISH DATE ....

☆☆☆☆☆

PLOT

THOUGHTS

QUOTES

Book Review

TITLE ....

AUTHOR ....

SERIES ....

SERIES BOOK # .... PAGE COUNT ....

GENRE ....

FORMAT ....

START DATE .... FINISH DATE ....

☆☆☆☆☆

PLOT

_____

THOUGHTS

_____

QUOTES

Book Review

TITLE ....

AUTHOR ....

SERIES..

SERIES BOOK #.............. PAGE COUNT................

GENRE...

FORMAT...

START DATE................. FINISH DATE ....

☆☆☆☆☆

PLOT

THOUGHTS

QUOTES

Book Review

TITLE ....

AUTHOR ....

SERIES ....

SERIES BOOK # .... PAGE COUNT ....

GENRE ....

FORMAT ....

START DATE .... FINISH DATE ....

☆☆☆☆☆

PLOT

THOUGHTS

QUOTES

Book Review

TITLE ....

AUTHOR ....

SERIES...

SERIES BOOK #............. PAGE COUNT...............

GENRE..

FORMAT...

START DATE................ FINISH DATE ....

☆☆☆☆☆

PLOT

THOUGHTS

QUOTES

Book Review

TITLE ....

AUTHOR ....

SERIES...

SERIES BOOK #.............. PAGE COUNT...............

GENRE..

FORMAT...

START DATE................. FINISH DATE ....

☆☆☆☆☆

PLOT

THOUGHTS

QUOTES

Book Review

TITLE ....

AUTHOR ....

SERIES...

SERIES BOOK #................. PAGE COUNT..................

GENRE...

FORMAT...

START DATE................... FINISH DATE ....

☆☆☆☆☆

PLOT

THOUGHTS

QUOTES

Book Review

TITLE ....

AUTHOR ....

SERIES..

SERIES BOOK #............... PAGE COUNT...............

GENRE...

FORMAT..

START DATE................. FINISH DATE ....

☆☆☆☆☆

PLOT

_____

THOUGHTS

_____

QUOTES

Book Review

TITLE ....

AUTHOR ....

SERIES..

SERIES BOOK # .... PAGE COUNT................

GENRE...

FORMAT...

START DATE.................. FINISH DATE ....

☆☆☆☆☆

PLOT

THOUGHTS

QUOTES

Book Review

TITLE ....

AUTHOR ....

SERIES ....

SERIES BOOK # .... PAGE COUNT ....

GENRE ....

FORMAT ....

START DATE .... FINISH DATE ....

☆☆☆☆☆

PLOT

THOUGHTS

QUOTES

Book Review

TITLE ....

AUTHOR ....

SERIES..

SERIES BOOK #............... PAGE COUNT................

GENRE...

FORMAT...

START DATE.................. FINISH DATE ....

☆☆☆☆☆

PLOT

THOUGHTS

QUOTES

Book Review

TITLE ....

AUTHOR ....

SERIES..

SERIES BOOK #................ PAGE COUNT................

GENRE...

FORMAT...

START DATE.................. FINISH DATE ....

☆☆☆☆☆

PLOT

THOUGHTS

QUOTES

Book Review

TITLE ....

AUTHOR ....

SERIES..

SERIES BOOK #................ PAGE COUNT................

GENRE..

FORMAT...

START DATE................. FINISH DATE ....

PLOT

THOUGHTS

QUOTES

Book Review

TITLE ....

AUTHOR ....

SERIES...

SERIES BOOK #............... PAGE COUNT...............

GENRE..

FORMAT...

START DATE............... FINISH DATE ....

PLOT

THOUGHTS

QUOTES

Book Review

TITLE ....

AUTHOR ....

SERIES..

SERIES BOOK #............. PAGE COUNT...............

GENRE..

FORMAT...

START DATE................. FINISH DATE ....

PLOT

THOUGHTS

QUOTES

Book Review

TITLE ....

AUTHOR ....

SERIES...

SERIES BOOK #............... PAGE COUNT...............

GENRE..

FORMAT..

START DATE................. FINISH DATE ....

☆☆☆☆☆

PLOT

THOUGHTS

QUOTES

Book Review

TITLE ....

AUTHOR ....

SERIES..

SERIES BOOK #............... PAGE COUNT...............

GENRE..

FORMAT...

START DATE................ FINISH DATE ....

☆☆☆☆☆☆

PLOT

THOUGHTS

QUOTES

Book Review

TITLE ....

AUTHOR ....

SERIES...

SERIES BOOK #............. PAGE COUNT...............

GENRE..

FORMAT..

START DATE................. FINISH DATE ....

☆☆☆☆☆

PLOT

___

THOUGHTS

___

QUOTES

Book Review

TITLE ....

AUTHOR ....

SERIES...

SERIES BOOK #.............. PAGE COUNT...............

GENRE...

FORMAT..

START DATE................. FINISH DATE ....

☆☆☆☆☆

PLOT

THOUGHTS

QUOTES

Book Review

TITLE ....

AUTHOR ....

SERIES ....

SERIES BOOK # .... PAGE COUNT ....

GENRE ....

FORMAT ....

START DATE .... FINISH DATE ....

☆☆☆☆☆

PLOT

THOUGHTS

QUOTES

Book Review

TITLE ....

AUTHOR ....

SERIES ....

SERIES BOOK # .... PAGE COUNT ....

GENRE ....

FORMAT ....

START DATE .... FINISH DATE ....

☆☆☆☆☆

PLOT

THOUGHTS

QUOTES

Book Review

TITLE ....

AUTHOR ....

SERIES ....

SERIES BOOK # .... PAGE COUNT ....

GENRE ....

FORMAT ....

START DATE .... FINISH DATE ....

☆☆☆☆☆

PLOT

THOUGHTS

QUOTES

Book Review

TITLE ....

AUTHOR ....

SERIES ....

SERIES BOOK # .... PAGE COUNT ....

GENRE ....

FORMAT ....

START DATE .... FINISH DATE ....

☆☆☆☆☆

PLOT

THOUGHTS

QUOTES

Book Review

TITLE ....

AUTHOR ....

SERIES..

SERIES BOOK #............... PAGE COUNT................

GENRE..

FORMAT..

START DATE.................. FINISH DATE ....

PLOT

THOUGHTS

QUOTES

Book Review

TITLE ....

AUTHOR ....

SERIES...

SERIES BOOK #.............. PAGE COUNT................

GENRE..

FORMAT...

START DATE................. FINISH DATE ....

☆☆☆☆☆

PLOT

THOUGHTS

QUOTES

Book Review

TITLE ....

AUTHOR ....

SERIES..

SERIES BOOK #............... PAGE COUNT...............

GENRE...

FORMAT..

START DATE................. FINISH DATE ....

☆☆☆☆☆

PLOT

THOUGHTS

QUOTES

Book Review

TITLE ....

AUTHOR ....

SERIES..

SERIES BOOK #.............. PAGE COUNT..............

GENRE..

FORMAT...

START DATE................. FINISH DATE ....

☆☆☆☆☆

PLOT

THOUGHTS

QUOTES

Book Review

TITLE ....

AUTHOR ....

SERIES...

SERIES BOOK #.............. PAGE COUNT...............

GENRE..

FORMAT...

START DATE............... FINISH DATE ....

☆☆☆☆☆

PLOT

THOUGHTS

QUOTES

Book Review

TITLE ....

AUTHOR ....

SERIES...

SERIES BOOK #............. PAGE COUNT...............

GENRE...

FORMAT...

START DATE.................. FINISH DATE ....

☆☆☆☆☆

PLOT

THOUGHTS

QUOTES

Book Review

TITLE ....

AUTHOR ....

SERIES..

SERIES BOOK #................ PAGE COUNT...............

GENRE...

FORMAT...

START DATE.................. FINISH DATE ....

☆☆☆☆☆

PLOT

THOUGHTS

QUOTES

Book Review

TITLE ....

AUTHOR ....

SERIES...

SERIES BOOK #.............. PAGE COUNT................

GENRE...

FORMAT..

START DATE................. FINISH DATE ....

☆☆☆☆☆

PLOT

THOUGHTS

QUOTES

Book Review

TITLE ....

AUTHOR ....

SERIES...

SERIES BOOK #............. PAGE COUNT...............

GENRE...

FORMAT...

START DATE................ FINISH DATE ....

☆☆☆☆☆

PLOT

THOUGHTS

QUOTES

Book Review

TITLE ....

AUTHOR ....

SERIES..

SERIES BOOK #.............. PAGE COUNT...............

GENRE..

FORMAT...

START DATE................ FINISH DATE ....

☆☆☆☆☆

PLOT

THOUGHTS

QUOTES

Book Review

TITLE ....

AUTHOR ....

SERIES..

SERIES BOOK #............ PAGE COUNT............

GENRE...

FORMAT..

START DATE............... FINISH DATE ....

☆☆☆☆☆

PLOT

THOUGHTS

QUOTES

Book Review

TITLE ....

AUTHOR ....

SERIES..

SERIES BOOK #.............. PAGE COUNT...............

GENRE..

FORMAT..

START DATE................. FINISH DATE ....

☆☆☆☆☆

PLOT

THOUGHTS

QUOTES

Book Review

TITLE ....

AUTHOR ....

SERIES..

SERIES BOOK #............... PAGE COUNT...............

GENRE...

FORMAT..

START DATE................. FINISH DATE ....

☆☆☆☆☆

PLOT

THOUGHTS

QUOTES

Book Review

TITLE ....

AUTHOR ....

SERIES ....

SERIES BOOK # .... PAGE COUNT ....

GENRE ....

FORMAT ....

START DATE .... FINISH DATE ....

☆☆☆☆☆

PLOT

THOUGHTS

QUOTES

Book Review

TITLE ....

AUTHOR ....

SERIES ....

SERIES BOOK # .... PAGE COUNT ....

GENRE ....

FORMAT ....

START DATE .... FINISH DATE ....

☆ ☆ ☆ ☆ ☆

PLOT

THOUGHTS

QUOTES

Book Review

TITLE ....

AUTHOR ....

SERIES...

SERIES BOOK #............... PAGE COUNT................

GENRE...

FORMAT...

START DATE................. FINISH DATE ....

☆☆☆☆☆

PLOT

THOUGHTS

QUOTES

Book Review

TITLE ....

AUTHOR ....

SERIES...

SERIES BOOK #.............. PAGE COUNT..............

GENRE...

FORMAT...

START DATE................ FINISH DATE ....

☆☆☆☆☆

PLOT

THOUGHTS

QUOTES

Book Review

TITLE ....

AUTHOR ....

SERIES...

SERIES BOOK #............. PAGE COUNT...............

GENRE...

FORMAT...

START DATE................ FINISH DATE ....

☆☆☆☆☆

PLOT

THOUGHTS

QUOTES

Book Review

TITLE ....

AUTHOR ....

SERIES..

SERIES BOOK #............. PAGE COUNT.............

GENRE..

FORMAT..

START DATE................. FINISH DATE ....

☆☆☆☆☆

PLOT

_____

THOUGHTS

_____

QUOTES

Book Review

TITLE ....

AUTHOR ....

SERIES...

SERIES BOOK #............... PAGE COUNT..................

GENRE..

FORMAT...

START DATE.................. FINISH DATE ....

☆☆☆☆☆

PLOT

THOUGHTS

QUOTES

Book Review

TITLE ....

AUTHOR ....

SERIES..

SERIES BOOK #............... PAGE COUNT...............

GENRE..

FORMAT..

START DATE................. FINISH DATE ....

☆☆☆☆☆

PLOT

THOUGHTS

QUOTES

Book Review

TITLE ....

AUTHOR ....

SERIES...

SERIES BOOK #............ PAGE COUNT...........

GENRE..

FORMAT...

START DATE................ FINISH DATE ....

☆☆☆☆☆

PLOT

THOUGHTS

QUOTES

Book Review

TITLE ....

AUTHOR ....

SERIES...

SERIES BOOK #............. PAGE COUNT.............

GENRE..

FORMAT..

START DATE................. FINISH DATE ....

☆☆☆☆☆

PLOT

THOUGHTS

QUOTES

Book Review

TITLE ....

AUTHOR ....

SERIES...

SERIES BOOK #............. PAGE COUNT.............

GENRE...

FORMAT...

START DATE................. FINISH DATE ....

☆☆☆☆☆

PLOT

THOUGHTS

QUOTES

Book Review

TITLE ....

AUTHOR ....

SERIES...

SERIES BOOK #.............. PAGE COUNT..............

GENRE..

FORMAT..

START DATE................ FINISH DATE ....

☆☆☆☆☆

PLOT

THOUGHTS

QUOTES

Book Review

TITLE ....

AUTHOR ....

SERIES...

SERIES BOOK #.............. PAGE COUNT..............

GENRE...

FORMAT...

START DATE................. FINISH DATE ....

☆☆☆☆☆

PLOT

THOUGHTS

QUOTES

Book Review

TITLE ....

AUTHOR ....

SERIES...

SERIES BOOK #............. PAGE COUNT...............

GENRE..

FORMAT...

START DATE................ FINISH DATE ....

☆☆☆☆☆

PLOT

THOUGHTS

QUOTES

Book Review

TITLE ....

AUTHOR ....

SERIES...

SERIES BOOK #............. PAGE COUNT..............

GENRE..

FORMAT..

START DATE................. FINISH DATE ....

☆☆☆☆☆

PLOT

THOUGHTS

QUOTES

Book Review

TITLE ....

AUTHOR ....

SERIES ....

SERIES BOOK # .... PAGE COUNT ....

GENRE ....

FORMAT ....

START DATE .... FINISH DATE ....

☆☆☆☆☆

PLOT

_____

THOUGHTS

_____

QUOTES

Book Review

TITLE ....

AUTHOR ....

SERIES...

SERIES BOOK #.............. PAGE COUNT..............

GENRE..

FORMAT..

START DATE................. FINISH DATE ....

PLOT

THOUGHTS

QUOTES

Book Review

TITLE ....

AUTHOR ....

SERIES ....

SERIES BOOK # .... PAGE COUNT ....

GENRE ....

FORMAT ....

START DATE .... FINISH DATE ....

☆☆☆☆☆

PLOT

THOUGHTS

QUOTES

Book Review

TITLE ....

AUTHOR ....

SERIES...

SERIES BOOK #............ PAGE COUNT...............

GENRE...

FORMAT..

START DATE................ FINISH DATE ....

☆☆☆☆☆

PLOT

THOUGHTS

QUOTES

Book Review

TITLE ....

AUTHOR ....

SERIES..

SERIES BOOK #.............. PAGE COUNT.................

GENRE...

FORMAT...

START DATE................. FINISH DATE ....

☆☆☆☆☆

PLOT

THOUGHTS

QUOTES

Book Review

TITLE ....

AUTHOR ....

SERIES..

SERIES BOOK #............. PAGE COUNT.................

GENRE..

FORMAT...

START DATE................. FINISH DATE ....

☆☆☆☆☆

PLOT

_____

THOUGHTS

_____

QUOTES

Book Review

TITLE ....

AUTHOR ....

SERIES ....

SERIES BOOK # .... PAGE COUNT ....

GENRE ....

FORMAT ....

START DATE .... FINISH DATE ....

☆☆☆☆☆

PLOT

THOUGHTS

QUOTES

Book Review

TITLE ....

AUTHOR ....

SERIES...

SERIES BOOK #............. PAGE COUNT...............

GENRE...

FORMAT...

START DATE................. FINISH DATE ....

☆☆☆☆☆

PLOT

THOUGHTS

QUOTES

Book Review

TITLE ....

AUTHOR ....

SERIES ....

SERIES BOOK # .... PAGE COUNT ....

GENRE ....

FORMAT ....

START DATE .... FINISH DATE ....

☆☆☆☆☆

PLOT

THOUGHTS

QUOTES

Book Review

TITLE ....

AUTHOR ....

SERIES..

SERIES BOOK #............... PAGE COUNT...............

GENRE..

FORMAT...

START DATE................ FINISH DATE ....

☆☆☆☆☆

PLOT

THOUGHTS

QUOTES

Book Review

TITLE ....

AUTHOR ....

SERIES..

SERIES BOOK #................. PAGE COUNT...............

GENRE...

FORMAT..

START DATE................. FINISH DATE ....

☆☆☆☆☆

PLOT

THOUGHTS

QUOTES

Book Review

TITLE ....

AUTHOR ....

SERIES...

SERIES BOOK #............. PAGE COUNT...............

GENRE...

FORMAT...

START DATE................. FINISH DATE ....

☆ ☆ ☆ ☆ ☆

PLOT

THOUGHTS

QUOTES

Book Review

TITLE ....

AUTHOR ....

SERIES...

SERIES BOOK #.............. PAGE COUNT...............

GENRE...

FORMAT..

START DATE................ FINISH DATE ....

☆☆☆☆☆

PLOT

THOUGHTS

QUOTES

Book Review

TITLE ....

AUTHOR ....

SERIES ....

SERIES BOOK # .... PAGE COUNT ....

GENRE ....

FORMAT ....

START DATE .... FINISH DATE ....

☆☆☆☆☆

PLOT

THOUGHTS

QUOTES

Book Review

TITLE ....

AUTHOR ....

SERIES ....

SERIES BOOK # .... PAGE COUNT ....

GENRE ....

FORMAT ....

START DATE .... FINISH DATE ....

☆☆☆☆☆

PLOT

THOUGHTS

QUOTES

Book Review

TITLE ....

AUTHOR ....

SERIES ....

SERIES BOOK #............. PAGE COUNT..............

GENRE ....

FORMAT..

START DATE................. FINISH DATE ....

☆☆☆☆☆

PLOT

THOUGHTS

QUOTES

Book Review

TITLE ....

AUTHOR ....

SERIES...

SERIES BOOK #.............. PAGE COUNT..............

GENRE...

FORMAT...

START DATE................. FINISH DATE ....

☆☆☆☆☆

PLOT

THOUGHTS

QUOTES

Book Review

TITLE ....

AUTHOR ....

SERIES..

SERIES BOOK #............. PAGE COUNT.............

GENRE...

FORMAT...

START DATE.............. FINISH DATE ....

PLOT

THOUGHTS

QUOTES

Book Review

TITLE ....

AUTHOR ....

SERIES ....

SERIES BOOK # .... PAGE COUNT ....

GENRE ....

FORMAT ....

START DATE .... FINISH DATE ....

☆☆☆☆☆

PLOT

THOUGHTS

QUOTES

Book Review

TITLE ....

AUTHOR ....

SERIES...

SERIES BOOK #.............. PAGE COUNT...............

GENRE...

FORMAT..

START DATE................. FINISH DATE ....

☆☆☆☆☆

PLOT

THOUGHTS

QUOTES

Book Review

TITLE ....

AUTHOR ....

SERIES..

SERIES BOOK #............. PAGE COUNT..............

GENRE...

FORMAT..

START DATE............... FINISH DATE ....

PLOT

THOUGHTS

QUOTES

Book Review

TITLE ....

AUTHOR ....

SERIES..

SERIES BOOK #.............. PAGE COUNT...............

GENRE..

FORMAT..

START DATE.................. FINISH DATE ....

☆☆☆☆☆

PLOT

_____

THOUGHTS

_____

QUOTES

Book Review

TITLE ....

AUTHOR ....

SERIES...

SERIES BOOK #.............. PAGE COUNT..............

GENRE..

FORMAT..

START DATE............... FINISH DATE ....

☆☆☆☆☆

PLOT

THOUGHTS

QUOTES

Book Review

TITLE ....

AUTHOR ....

SERIES..

SERIES BOOK #............... PAGE COUNT...............

GENRE..

FORMAT...

START DATE.................. FINISH DATE ....

☆☆☆☆☆

PLOT

THOUGHTS

QUOTES

Book Review

TITLE ....

AUTHOR ....

SERIES ....

SERIES BOOK # .... PAGE COUNT ....

GENRE ....

FORMAT ....

START DATE .... FINISH DATE ....

☆ ☆ ☆ ☆ ☆

PLOT

THOUGHTS

QUOTES

Book Review

TITLE ....

AUTHOR ....

SERIES...

SERIES BOOK #.............. PAGE COUNT................

GENRE...

FORMAT...

START DATE................. FINISH DATE ....

☆☆☆☆☆

PLOT

THOUGHTS

QUOTES

Book Review

TITLE ....

AUTHOR ....

SERIES...

SERIES BOOK #.............. PAGE COUNT..............

GENRE..

FORMAT..

START DATE.............. FINISH DATE ....

☆☆☆☆☆

PLOT

THOUGHTS

QUOTES

Book Review

TITLE ....

AUTHOR ....

SERIES ....

SERIES BOOK # .... PAGE COUNT ....

GENRE ....

FORMAT ....

START DATE .... FINISH DATE ....

☆☆☆☆☆

PLOT

THOUGHTS

QUOTES

Book Review

TITLE ....

AUTHOR ....

SERIES...

SERIES BOOK #............... PAGE COUNT...............

GENRE...

FORMAT...

 START DATE................ FINISH DATE ....

☆ ☆ ☆ ☆ ☆

PLOT

THOUGHTS

QUOTES

Book Review

TITLE ....

AUTHOR ....

SERIES ....

SERIES BOOK # .... PAGE COUNT ....

GENRE ....

FORMAT ....

START DATE .... FINISH DATE ....

☆☆☆☆☆

PLOT

THOUGHTS

QUOTES

Book Review

TITLE ....

AUTHOR ....

SERIES..

SERIES BOOK #.............. PAGE COUNT...............

GENRE...

FORMAT..

START DATE................ FINISH DATE ....

☆☆☆☆☆

PLOT

_____

THOUGHTS

_____

QUOTES

Book Review

TITLE ....

AUTHOR ....

SERIES..

SERIES BOOK #.............. PAGE COUNT................

GENRE...

FORMAT..

START DATE................. FINISH DATE ....

☆☆☆☆☆

PLOT

THOUGHTS

QUOTES

Book Review

TITLE ....

AUTHOR ....

SERIES...

SERIES BOOK #............. PAGE COUNT...............

GENRE...

FORMAT..

START DATE................ FINISH DATE ....

☆☆☆☆☆

PLOT

THOUGHTS

QUOTES

Book Review

TITLE ....

AUTHOR ....

SERIES...

SERIES BOOK #............... PAGE COUNT..............

GENRE...

FORMAT...

START DATE............... FINISH DATE ....

☆☆☆☆☆

PLOT

THOUGHTS

QUOTES

Book Review

TITLE ....

AUTHOR ....

SERIES..

SERIES BOOK #............... PAGE COUNT...............

GENRE..

FORMAT...

START DATE................. FINISH DATE ....

☆☆☆☆☆

PLOT

THOUGHTS

QUOTES

Book Review

TITLE ....

AUTHOR ....

SERIES...

SERIES BOOK #................. PAGE COUNT...............

GENRE...

FORMAT...

START DATE................. FINISH DATE ....

☆☆☆☆☆

PLOT

THOUGHTS

QUOTES

Book Review

TITLE ....

AUTHOR ....

SERIES...

SERIES BOOK #.............. PAGE COUNT...............

GENRE..

FORMAT...

START DATE................ FINISH DATE ....

PLOT

THOUGHTS

QUOTES

Book Review

TITLE ....
AUTHOR ....
SERIES...
SERIES BOOK #............... PAGE COUNT.................
GENRE..
FORMAT...
START DATE................. FINISH DATE ....

☆☆☆☆☆

PLOT

THOUGHTS

QUOTES

Book Review

TITLE ....

AUTHOR ....

SERIES..

SERIES BOOK #.............. PAGE COUNT.................

GENRE...

FORMAT..

START DATE................ FINISH DATE ....

PLOT

THOUGHTS

QUOTES

Book Review

TITLE ....

AUTHOR ....

SERIES..

SERIES BOOK #............. PAGE COUNT...............

GENRE...

FORMAT...

START DATE.................. FINISH DATE ....

☆☆☆☆☆

PLOT

THOUGHTS

QUOTES

Book Review

TITLE ....

AUTHOR ....

SERIES..

SERIES BOOK #.............. PAGE COUNT................

GENRE...

FORMAT...

START DATE................. FINISH DATE ....

☆☆☆☆☆

PLOT

THOUGHTS

QUOTES

Book Review

TITLE ....

AUTHOR ....

SERIES...

SERIES BOOK #............. PAGE COUNT.................

GENRE..

FORMAT...

START DATE................. FINISH DATE ....

☆☆☆☆☆

PLOT

THOUGHTS

QUOTES

Book Review

TITLE ....

AUTHOR ....

SERIES..

SERIES BOOK #.............. PAGE COUNT...............

GENRE...

FORMAT..

START DATE................. FINISH DATE ....

☆☆☆☆☆

PLOT

THOUGHTS

QUOTES

Book Review

TITLE ....

AUTHOR ....

SERIES...

SERIES BOOK #............. PAGE COUNT...............

GENRE...

FORMAT...

START DATE................. FINISH DATE ....

☆ ☆ ☆ ☆ ☆

PLOT

_____

THOUGHTS

_____

QUOTES

Book Review

TITLE ....

AUTHOR ....

SERIES...

SERIES BOOK #.............. PAGE COUNT...............

GENRE...

FORMAT..

START DATE.............. FINISH DATE ....

☆☆☆☆☆

PLOT

THOUGHTS

QUOTES

Book Review

TITLE ....

AUTHOR ....

SERIES...

SERIES BOOK #.............. PAGE COUNT................

GENRE...

FORMAT...

START DATE.................. FINISH DATE ....

☆☆☆☆☆

PLOT

THOUGHTS

QUOTES

Book Review

TITLE ....

AUTHOR ....

SERIES..

SERIES BOOK #.............. PAGE COUNT...............

GENRE...

FORMAT...

START DATE................. FINISH DATE ....

☆☆☆☆☆

PLOT

THOUGHTS

QUOTES

Book Review

TITLE ....

AUTHOR ....

SERIES..

SERIES BOOK #............... PAGE COUNT...............

GENRE..

FORMAT..

START DATE................ FINISH DATE ....

☆☆☆☆☆

PLOT

THOUGHTS

QUOTES

Book Review

TITLE ....

AUTHOR ....

SERIES...

SERIES BOOK #............ PAGE COUNT...............

GENRE...

FORMAT..

START DATE.............. FINISH DATE ....

☆☆☆☆☆

PLOT

THOUGHTS

QUOTES

Book Review

TITLE ....

AUTHOR ....

SERIES ....

SERIES BOOK # .... PAGE COUNT ....

GENRE ....

FORMAT ....

START DATE .... FINISH DATE ....

☆☆☆☆☆

PLOT

THOUGHTS

QUOTES

Book Review

TITLE ....

AUTHOR ....

SERIES..

SERIES BOOK #.............. PAGE COUNT...............

GENRE..

FORMAT..

 START DATE............... FINISH DATE ....

☆☆☆☆☆

PLOT

THOUGHTS

QUOTES

Book Review

TITLE ....

AUTHOR ....

SERIES..

SERIES BOOK #............... PAGE COUNT...............

GENRE...

FORMAT..

START DATE................. FINISH DATE ....

☆☆☆☆☆

PLOT

THOUGHTS

QUOTES

Book Review

TITLE ....

AUTHOR ....

SERIES ....

SERIES BOOK # .... PAGE COUNT ....

GENRE ....

FORMAT ....

START DATE .... FINISH DATE ....

☆ ☆ ☆ ☆ ☆

PLOT

THOUGHTS

QUOTES

Book Review

TITLE ....

AUTHOR ....

SERIES...

SERIES BOOK #.............. PAGE COUNT..............

GENRE...

FORMAT...

START DATE................. FINISH DATE ....

☆☆☆☆☆

PLOT

_____

THOUGHTS

_____

QUOTES

Made in the USA
Monee, IL
10 February 2022

c93c2bb9-06c6-4767-9cf0-eedadce57102R01